FOLLOW THE YELLOW BRICK ROAD WITH CIA

ANTHONY JONES

A Pen Press Publication

© Anthony Jones 2009

All rights reserved

No part of this publication may be reproduced, stored in a retrieval system, or transmitted in any form or by any means, without the prior permission in writing of the publisher, nor be otherwise circulated in any form of binding or cover other than that in which it is published and without a similar condition including this condition being imposed on the subsequent purchaser.

First published in Great Britain by Pen Press

All paper used in the printing of this book has been made from wood grown in managed, sustainable forests.

ISBN13: 978-1-906206-98-7

Printed and bound in the UK
Pen Press is an imprint of Indepenpress Publishing Limited
25 Eastern Place
Brighton
BN2 1GJ

A catalogue record of this book is available from
the British Library

Cover design by Jacqueline Abromeit

INTRODUCTION

This book is designed to help those who wish to become more likeable, more lovable and more capable.

When we enter this fascinating world we are usually loving, friendly and trusting. The birds sing and the sun shines on our needy, demanding innocence. But gradually we are transformed: we discover that some adults do not understand us; we have to compete and we have to share, but worst of all, our friendly feelings are not always welcomed. Because of this we may become resentful, hostile or defensively withdrawn; reactions that may make us less likeable and less lovable. But in many cases false impressions about ourselves and others can be remedied.

FOLLOW THE YELLOW BRICK ROAD WITH CIA contains a formula for specifying and coping with psychological and emotional problems.

DNA, it is said, is the modern version of the soul. Genes, it is believed, can influence behaviour. If these beliefs are true, action needs to be taken to curb further impediments to self-assertion such as harmful addictions, peer pressure, faulty upbringing, and thoughtless commitment to hand-me-down beliefs.

Although organised religion in the West is no longer the force it once was, it can still obstruct self-determination and free thinking. If people are deprived of the capacity to live their own life due to imposed indoctrination, whether political or religious, individuality and choice may thereby be virtually surrendered. For this reason due attention is given in this book to self-assertion and awareness.

Auto-suggestion has a long history, predating language and thought. Animals use an instinctive form of auto-suggestion by means of desire, need, willpower, pictorial memory and intense concentration as they predetermine the death of their prey. Our inheritance of these primitive powers enables us through language and thought to strengthen will and determination while in pursuit of various objectives.

Stigmatic personalities demonstrate these powers when they replicate upon themselves the wounds inflicted on Christ during his crucifixion – a graphic example of mind over matter.

Special attention is given to the power and use of auto-suggestion as a means of promoting confidence and positive attitudes. Many wonderfully inventive and adventurous Victorians attached slogans to their walls, giving guidelines and reminders relating to virtues, aims and resolutions that probably inspired them to endure the grinding toil and poverty of the Industrial Revolution era. In this millennium readers may also get support from slogans (the sort printed herein) that are appropriate to daily endeavours.

In relation to sanity and ethics the role played by ancient Greeks such as Socrates is respectfully acknowledged.

PREFACE

Life is like a busy railway station;
people are continually coming or going;
but despite all the hustle and bustle
and frantic efforts to succeed

you should never be too busy
to pause when yellow striped bumble bees
hover and buzz over a
red, red rose,

or when spray-spattered gulls
send out their mournful cry
as they dive and whirl to the
blustery roar of a raging sea,

because the station master's waiting,
as he glances at the time,
to guide you on your journey
to the end of the line.

(Anthony Jones)

To Joanne and Susie and to the memory of Irene

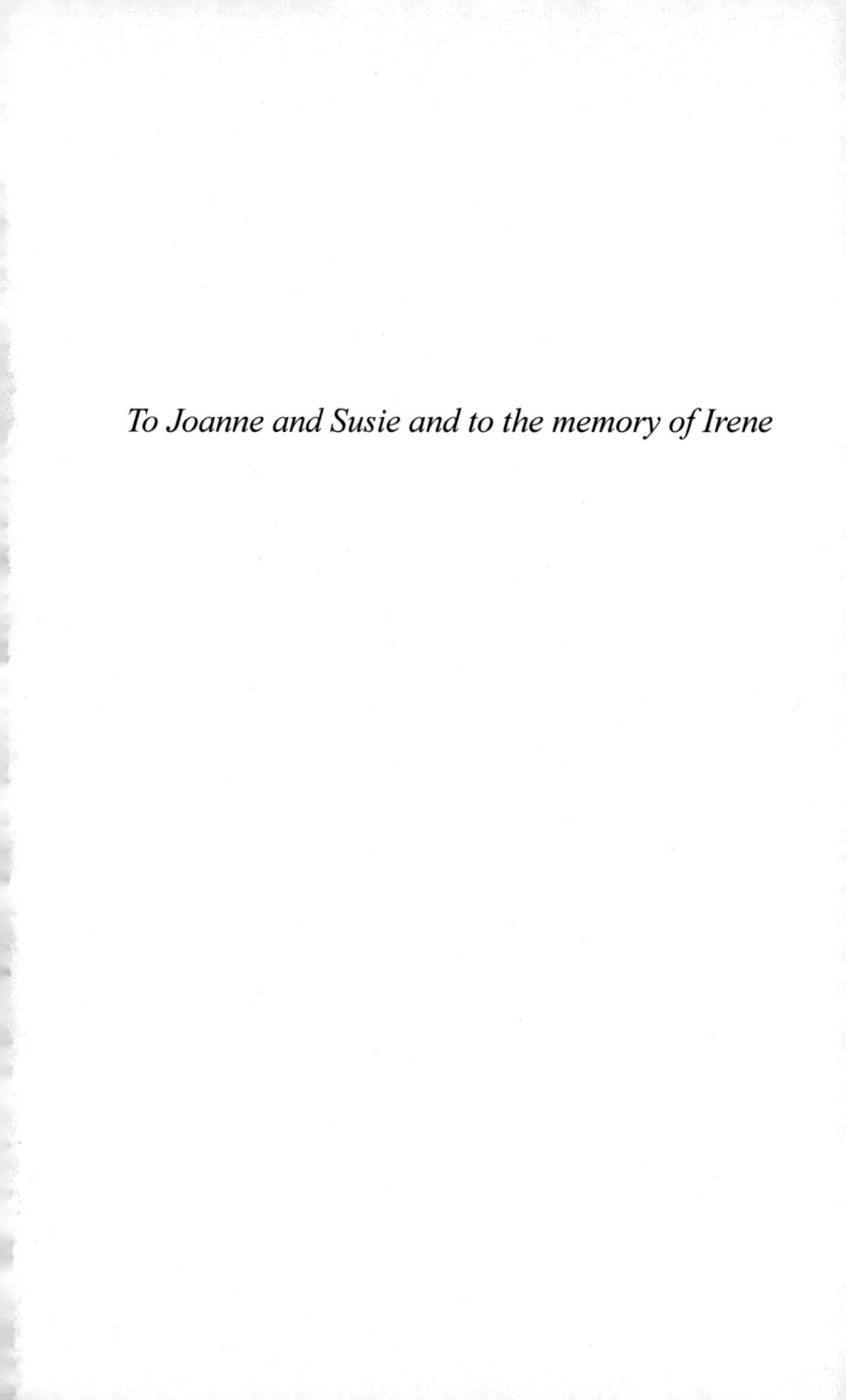

CONTENTS

Introduction iii
Preface v

PART ONE
Follow the Yellow Brick Road with CIA 1
The system and the aims 3
What self-help psychotherapy may do for you 4
How we reveal ourselves 7
Psychotherapy 11
Who needs psychotherapy? 13
Icons of psychotherapy 15
Reaching the unconscious aspect of your mind 21
Confidence 26
C I A 30
The burden of habitual pretence 32

The zones of experience 34
The red zone 36
Common causes of discontent in the red zone 37
Tackling a cause of discontent 39
Is fear keeping you in the red zone? 40
Fear of taking a risk 42
Dealing with unreasonable fears 45
The amber zone 46

Chekhov's three sisters in the amber zone 47
Loneliness 49
Friendships: in the give and take of life 57
It's getting easier and more enjoyable to talk to people .. 59
Awareness in the amber zone 60
Self-analysis through self awareness 63
The green zone 66
Emotional intelligence 67

PART TWO
Action through thought control 71
Feeling socially at-ease 73
Acting responsibly 76
Our animal heritage 78
Stigmata and auto-suggestion 81
Action - determining future events 86
Should we force-feed on new experiences? 88
Ways of overcoming emotional stalemate 90

PART THREE
Psychological and emotional insight
Aspects of love 99
A kind of loving 101
Signs and consequences of low self-esteem 107
Psychological insight into low self-esteem. 109
Insights and feelings 112
In fear of love 118
Barriers to likeability and lovability 120
Transcendental absolution from anti-social feelings 125
Overcoming negative stress 127
Peace of mind in 100 seconds 130
Stress and capability 132
Boredom and stress 134

Harmful prenatal influences 136
Social influences on children 138
Obesity 140
Influencing your lifespan 145
The return of Diego Maradona 146
Influencing your child's lifespan 149
The powers of a baby 151
Marriage or cohabitation 156

PART FOUR
Self determination
Have you surrendered your mind? 165
The great divide that threatens world peace 169
Handing over your mind to brainwashers 172
Self-determination and personal responsibility 175
Genetic barriers to self-determination 178
Influences that can affect capability 181
Drug addiction 185
Drugs in the workplace: the effects on capability
and the value of self-awareness 187
Drugs in the home 189
Sleep capability and memory 193
Agoraphobia and capability 194
The mind and the soul 196
Doing it your way 200
Materialism and ethics 204
Morality and chimpanzees 206
Standards of acceptable conduct 208
Materialism 210
Would a world without religion be safer and
more peaceful? 212
The Three Graces - Faith, Hope and Charity 214
Does Life Have a Purpose? 219

Choosing a Suitable Partner 228

PART FIVE
The best way to live 235
A portrait of a popular and positive person 238
Popularity and character 241
Humour and popularity 244
Encouraging words 247
Advice from Robert Louis Stevenson 248

PART ONE

FOLLOW THE YELLOW BRICK ROAD WITH CIA

In Frank Baum's masterpiece *The Wizard of Oz*, the Tin Woodman who needed a heart, the Scarecrow who needed a brain and the Lion who needed courage were accompanied by Dorothy and her dog Toto as they made their way along the yellow brick road that led to the Emerald City. Their purpose was to visit the Wizard of Oz who, they believed, could use his legendary powers to get them what they wanted more than anything in the world. When they eventually reached the Emerald City, they were assured by the fake wizard that their problems would be magically solved.

'It was easy to convince them of my magical powers,' said the wizard, 'because they believed I could do anything.' Although he wasn't a genuine wizard, he was well aware of the combined power of imagination, self-belief and suggestion.

Unlike those optimistic travellers, most people are forced to realise, as life progresses, that they alone can provide the necessary courage, insight and action to make their aims and wishes come true.

This book yields a formula and a system to guide travellers along life's symbolic yellow brick road which passes through zones of experience characterised by:
1. Confusion and despair
2. Realisation and intent.
3. A zone in which positive actions are taken to resolve problems.

THE SYSTEM AND THE AIMS

There are so many references in this book to likeability, lovability and capability that LLoC, an abbreviation of these qualities, is necessary:

L is likeability
Lo is lovability
C is capability

Capability can be enhanced by popularity that often stems from being likeable: likeable people are inclined, on the whole, to be more amiable in the work place and more effective in matters pertaining to public relations. Those who have achieved L and Lo through psychological and emotional insight - or a favourable upbringing - are less likely to make rash, emotional decisions or resort to damaging addictions; although of course there are exceptions to this generalisation.

WHAT SELF-HELP PSYCHOTHERAPY MAY DO FOR YOU

- Increase your willingness to take reasonable risks socially, emotionally and at work and become more confident about responsibilities.
- Enable you to become less likely to fear rejection or failure.
- Raise hopes and expectations as you reduce unnecessary fears and take a more positive attitude to life.
- Encourage self-belief so that you become socially more acceptable.
- Improve self-knowledge and your understanding of people and their problems as you become less self-centred.
- Enable you to recognise and cope with psychological and emotional barriers to aims, hopes and desires.
- Help you to become more aware of the *real you*, take greater control of your life and, partly through auto-suggestions, change what needs to be changed.
- Help you if you wish, to become more likeable, more lovable and more capable.

Although autosuggestions in relation to the above issues are prominently featured in this book, it should be pointed out that, effective though they can be in certain situations, they should ideally be used alongside emotional realisations connected with problems, conflicts and character adjustments.

Emotional realisations can arise from thoughts such as:

> Why am I afraid of emotional commitment?
> What memories are linked to my lack of confidence?
> What do I value most of all, and what is stopping me from attaining my desire? Is it lack of courage and self-belief?
> Am I really scared of rejection and failure? If so, why?
> Am I too self-centred and insecure to be sociable?
> Am I jealous?
> Am I a perfectionist because I feel so unacceptable?
> When did I last do somebody a good turn?

A psychotherapist, when applying psychoanalysis, would probably probe patiently for answers to questions like these. But being your own therapist means you are responsible for probing inside yourself for answers to the way you think and feel by using meditation, free association, dream association and dream interpretation. But in addition to these methods of gaining personal insight into the reasons behind inner conflict and general discontent, don't forget the value of talking things over with friends or colleagues; after all, they almost certainly have problems, too.

By analysing yourself from an ethical point of view, you may have to admit that you are as likely as anyone else to have repressed anger, envy or guilt. These human frailties need to be uncovered as they can be responsible for low self-esteem.

A thing that is worth having is worthy striving for; self-knowledge can set you free and bring peace of mind. The price you may need to pay is determination, a genuine effort to improve on attitudes and a more analytical approach towards the impact you have on other people.

HOW WE REVEAL OURSELVES

The renowned philosopher and psychologist Jesus Christ is reported to have said: 'By their deeds you shall know them' or words to that effect; and who can argue with that?

Ranting and raging
There are some fairly obvious ways of revealing the hidden *you.* For instance, if you continually rant and rage there has to be a cause or reason. Counselling or Psychotherapy may help to find an answer to behaviour which is often related to the sorts of frustrations that can make babies go red in the face when they feel powerless to make you understand what they want or how they feel.

Being unsociable or anti social may be due to current affronts to your self-esteem, lack of affection in childhood, a disinclination to make friends and social commitments in case you get disappointed or rejected, or a feeling that nobody would really like to know you anyway. Hopefully, this book will help to increase your self-esteem and provide appropriate insights into social attitudes.
If you are defensively aggressive or very critical of others, it may be a reflection of the way your parents treated you; we do tend to imitate them, often without realising it. One target of this book is to encourage the discovery of the

real you so that you are not burdened with hand-me-down attitudes and habits unconsciously adopted.

Lack of confidence and self-assertion can render a person as static as a car without petrol. There can, of course, be numerous reasons for a timid attitude to life, one of the most common being lack of self-belief. Anything that shatters a person's sense of worth by unkind remarks or unnecessary criticism is, in a way, robbing them of courage, of the strength to courageously assert themselves in relationships and life in general, especially if they already feel inadequate. And what is the magical ingredient that can foster confidence and moral courage in children and adults? The Beatles gave the answer: 'All you need is love'. Encouragement and kindness helps people to believe in themselves to a certain extent, as may the sorts of autosuggestions contained in this book, but achievements too can give a boost to the ego, however insignificant they may be. Asking someone for a dance instead of just watching others do it, opening up a conversation with a stranger or going after a job, knowing you may be disappointed, may seem trivial steps in the right direction, but you are likely to become increasingly bolder with practice. The attainment of knowledge and skills is of course important to the build-up of self esteem, and autosuggestions to increase confidence can help a great deal when hopeful ventures are attempted because a person needs to be psychologically and emotionally prepared to bounce back from disappointments that are inevitable from time to time. In this respect it is worth remembering the saying: 'If you haven't failed, then you haven't been trying hard enough or long enough.' One of several autosuggestions given in this book is 'I have the courage to face rejection and disappointments'. When you face life with this sort of attitude, you reveal yourself as someone who is prepared to take chances and have a go.

As self-knowledge increases, the personality you present to the world should become more balanced and you should be better equipped to assess the likely impact you may be having on other people and what measures you could take to improve your image.

If you are inclined to disregard other people's feelings, due to thinking too much about yourself – not acknowledging a smile or a 'good morning', for instance – it could be advisable to note that almost everybody wants and needs to be liked and respected. We do not usually like everybody but we can at least show respect; when we do, it is usually good for the other person's self-esteem and we are more likely to be respected in return. Lack of respect, (with respect defined as courtesy, consideration and good manners) may not be 'intended' to indicate that you hold someone in low regard but if the person who has been ignored or unintentionally by-passed lacks confidence or feels inferior, it may be seen or felt as such.

An inferiority complex is probably the most common and obvious way of revealing your inner self. One of the reasons is that people who feel inadequate often need to prove in a number of ways that they are not really inferior – by boasting; obsessive body-building; bullying; over-achieving; lying; fantasising; using alcohol or drugs as an escape from difficulties, imagined difficulties or a reality with which they cannot cope; exorbitant overdressing; violent, irrational behaviour; speaking too loudly; being over-sensitive to criticism; needing to be always right;

avoiding competitive situations or responsibilities; and in politics, a pursuit of power in order to compensate for feeling powerless. Being a constant attention-seeker is yet another revealing sign of emotional insecurity. Greed and miserliness are not always just about money and wealth; odd though it may seem, some people who appear prosperous and confident spend their lives accumulating riches so as to attain the security and respect they crave. Over-confidence and a pretentious accent may also be tell-tale signs of a sense of inferiority.

Self-analysis might indicate whether or not we attempt to *overcompensate* for feelings of inferiority: for example, criticising others so as to bring them down to our level, ostentatious behaviour, sarcasm or belittling people in some way. But dreams are one of the surest ways of revealing the person behind the mask.

It is comforting to reflect that hardly anybody manages completely to avoid revealing their inner selves. Perhaps all we can do is to minimise the negative give-aways as far as possible and maximise the better part of our nature. Many people are so self-critical that they forget or omit to take account of good characteristics such as generosity, patience, concern for the welfare of others or a tendency to be kind and encouraging.

PSYCHOTHERAPY
(Mind Healing)

Psychotherapy is not an exact science. This is borne out by the variety of mind therapies that exist.

Do-it-yourself psychotherapy includes features from four psychotherapy icons: Sigmund Freud, Carl Gustav Jung, Carl Rogers and Jean-Paul Sartre, however, this author puts additional emphasis on the powerful effect that words can have on emotions and imagination when expressed as suggestions and autosuggestions. A wad of appreciative letters supported by doctors' comments has proved to me how effective suggestive therapy can be. For example to encourage a person to become a more positive personality through repeated positive suggestions can sometimes over-ride lack of self-belief and lack of hope in a relatively short space of time.

Self-help psychotherapy tackles negative attitudes in two ways: by encouraging psychological and emotional insight, and through the power of autosuggestion.

*

Insight is achieved when the client understands the root of a conflict or problem and is then able to behave in an emotionally more mature manner.

*

Advertisers subtly coax most of us to spend our money through their repeated suggestions and related images. We can, through positive autosuggestions and imagination, use the same medium to influence ourselves in various ways, whether at a social gathering or making an important presentation at work. Several examples of self-assertive techniques are given throughout this book in appropriate sections.

WHO NEEDS PSYCHOTHERAPY?

Psychotherapy alone is not generally considered to be an appropriate method for the treatment of illnesses such as serious and prolonged mental depression, or psychosis in which thought and emotions are so impaired that perception of external reality is severely affected. These are conditions that usually necessitate the personal attention of a psychiatrist and /or medication.

But in the opinion of Carl Gustav Jung *'Psychotherapy transcends its medical origins and ceases to be merely a method of treating the sick. It now treats the healthy or such as has a moral right to psychic health, whose sickness is at most the suffering that torments us all'*.

The suffering that torments us all is writ large in daily newspapers throughout the world and in social statistics which bear out that fact that most of us need to understand ourselves and others a lot more if we wish to cope ably with life's problems. Self-help psychotherapy may make a useful contribution in this direction because it concentrates on the practicalities of improving life and can help people appreciate and maintain good mental health through the acquisition of self-knowledge.

Socrates the Greek philosopher did his best to spread understanding and tolerance. He seems to have spent much of his time helping people to be logical, understanding truth seekers able to make their own decisions after due consideration. In his opinion:

> *The unexamined life is not worth living.*
> *Ethical virtue is the only thing that really matters.*

Ethical virtues may not be in fashion nowadays but in support of Socrates' sentiments, so relative to a world beset by confusion and conflict, self-help psychotherapy as a means of self-knowledge does provide a system and method for the furtherance of spiritual and emotional growth in a changing world where doctrinaire inducements toward civility and morality appear to have become less effective.

The examined life

Although self-help psychotherapy can be effective in allaying domestic-based anxieties, many studies have shown that talk therapy plus anti-depressants can lead to significant improvement in most patients who suffer from illogical anxiety and day-to-day depression. Therefore, in places where people have no one to share their worries it may be advisable for them to contact their doctor or the social department of their local authority for group therapy, counselling or the setting up of talking groups.

This book relates 'the examined life' to a wide range of issues affecting the mind's interaction with emotions, body and spirit: as indicated by the list of contents.

ICONS OF PSYCHOTHERAPY

Two of the wisest people the world has ever known supported the following advice:
    Jesus Christ: Physician, Heal thyself.
    Socrates: Know thyself

Psychotherapy, assisted or of the self-help kind, is a means of acting on their words of wisdom in a practical, workable way.

Purportedly one in every four or five of the population needs mind-healing at some time in their life. Because of this huge demand, state-aided therapy resources are invariably overstretched, and many people cannot afford private treatment. But numerous problems can be overcome through self-understanding and productive adult relationships.

Psychoanalysis is no longer the only mind-healing treatment available. Many forms of psychotherapy have surfaced since Sigmund Freud added his unique approach to a deeper understanding of human behaviour. It could be said that J.S.Bach laid the foundation of classical music. It could also be said that Freud provided the basis from which various forms of psychotherapy have developed.

Sigmund Freud (1856-1939) introduced a method of treating mental disorders through the probing of unconscious processes. Some forms of psychotherapy are still based partially on some of his psychoanalytic techniques, one of which required patients to engage in free association of ideas:-

Free association, according to Freud, means speaking to a therapist about anything that comes into your mind.

In self-help psychotherapy if you are not sure what is worrying you, you can always avail yourself of free association, noting whatever comes into your mind just as people do who are meditating freely on past events. In this way you stand a chance of uncovering something that needs to be solved or acted upon: something you shoved into your mental dustbin because it was too inconvenient or difficult to cope with when it occurred. Freud found that in addition to free association, dreams and slips of the tongue could also provide clues to the workings of the unconscious mind. The aim of his type of psychotherapy is to uncover tensions between the instinctive drive (which he called the Id) and the censorship imposed by the morality of the superego (conscience) reflecting social standards learned from parents and teachers.

In Freudian analysis special attention is paid to early childhood experiences, particularly those of a sexual nature, the memory of which may have been repressed because of guilt or trauma (distress of some kind). Recalling and analysing these experiences is thought to help free patients from anxiety and neurosis caused by repression as well as from serious illnesses such as psychosis, a mental disorder in which thought and emotions are so impaired that perception of external reality is severely affected.

In modern times a common cause of self-imposed anxiety, neurosis and even psychosis is cannabis and other illicit drugs. It is not always acknowledged that alcohol addiction may also cause people to be similarly disorientated and dependent.

What is repression? *We forget or repress what we do not like or what is not socially acceptable, thereby expelling the thought or feeling from consciousness.*

Carl Gustav Jung (1875-1961), a one-time student and follower of Freud, was more in line with modern concepts of psychotherapy. Although he realised the importance of childhood experiences, Jung stressed the behavioural impact of day-to-day occurrences, especially when efforts to achieve are blocked or frustrated.

Jung differed from his mentor Freud on several issues, for example he was less interested in the past and more concerned with the present. Like Adler he saw the importance of self assertion: the goal to which a person is aiming.

He did agree with Freud that dreams are the royal road to the unconscious aspect of the mind, though he disagreed over the best way to interpret them. 'By freely associating on dream images,' he said, 'you run the risk of letting the dream image slip away. Free association, he maintained, will not explain the dream and may result in both patient and analyst failing to interpret it at all. If, on the other hand, you meditate on a dream sufficiently long and thoroughly, turning it over and over in your mind, something almost always comes of it. Jung's method appears to have prevailed.

If the puzzle of a dream is difficult to solve and you need to be concentrating on something else, try achieving remote control of the dream image by thinking 'I'll remember it.' Sure enough the unconscious will sometimes come up with the answer when you least expect it.

Instead of using Freud's term 'dream symbol', Jung preferred to say 'signs' because a symbol such as a dagger or umbrella could mean different things to different people. But despite differences of opinion on other issues, Jung appreciated the importance of Freud's seminal publication on The Interpretation of Dreams.

Carl Rogers (1902-87) is commonly associated with Humanistic Psychotherapy which stresses the individuality of human beings: that everyone has the potential for personal growth and the right to determine their own life; and that in pursuance of this they should face up to and try to overcome obstacles to personal growth such as negative attitudes, fears or cultural restrictions, for instance being trapped in the belief system one is given as a child. Rogers considered that a distressed person is more than the sum total of his or her problems.

Humanistic psychotherapy does not deal excessively

with childhood memories, as did Freud, and it does not give undue attention to spirituality, as some might say of Jung; but it does relate to mind, body emotions and spirit in the 'here and now' while also acknowledging that past influences can and do influence the present. Rogers pays particular attention to external factors that block the potential of human growth. An example of this involved the Japanese people, who had their growth potentialities blocked due to being conditioned to a belief that their emperor, Hirohito, was god-like – divine though in practice he merely ratified the policies formulated by his ministers and advisers. It was not until after WW2, in 1946, that their emperor repudiated his quasi-divine status. When the myth of his divinity was exposed, the Japanese people were surprisingly able to align themselves to Western realities of the 20th century: materialism, self-determination, freedom of choice and a fertile arena for personal growth.

Rogers encouraged counselling: person-to-person dialogue which can help clients to express their potential for coping with responsibilities while acquiring greater self realisation. Counselling also provides a talk situation, which may help to dissipate various domestic-based anxieties. This can be invaluable to people who have no one with whom they can discuss the source of their anxiety or depressive outlook: not even a husband or wife or partner.

Jean Paul Sartre (1905-80)
Sartre's humanistic, existential approach to therapy is a poison chalice for any dictator, political or religious, because broadly speaking, it encourages people to establish and value their true identity and make their own

decisions. If Paul Anker and the late Frank Sinatra had been apprehended in Europe during WW2 they would probably have been dealt with most severely because their song My Way dramatically proclaims the basics of Sartre's philosophy: freedom of choice, self-determination and defence of personal freedoms.

A tenet of existentialism is that because we are unsupported by any kind of extra-terrestrial largesse, we are left to make our own choices and bear responsibility for our own actions. A corollary of this self-sufficiency is that a certain amount of anxiety in an uncertain world is bound to arise but that is also true of guilt-laden religionists conditioned to believe in the myth of hell and damnation.

Ultimately, we have the choice (if we haven't been brainwashed) of finding enough spiritual strength from within ourselves to make a go of this life, or we can indolently permit some sect or religious dictatorship to do our thinking for us: rather like being under remote control. A great many religiously uncommitted people appear to blissfully rely on an imaginary god in the hope that somehow, somewhere we shall continue to exist after death in another form. But humanistic existentialists are prepared autonomously to be the captains of their ship and the masters of their souls.

REACHING THE UNCONSCIOUS ASPECT OF YOUR MIND

Peacefully consider why you have behaved irrationally as you allow your mind to wander back to a related situation. You may not trace a connection immediately but with patience and insistence a memory, possibly of an emotional nature, may jolt you into pertinent insight and hopefully enable you to avoid a recurrence of the same situation. This mental exercise necessitates the self-discipline of *making* time for meditation, no matter how busy your day may be. It really can be worth the effort because *if things don't alter they'll remain as they are* and that would not appear to be very productive in terms of personal growth.

- Excessive behaviour by other people may remind you how you have acted in similar circumstances: being unnecessarily disrespectful to a waiter, for instance.
- Reports and articles in newspapers, magazines and TV programmes can also jog people into greater awareness of biased or unreasonable attitudes and may occasionally trigger off feelings associated with repressed memories.
- Slips of the tongue – saying something you did

not intend to say can reveal your hidden thoughts and feelings.
- Critical remarks from relatives, friends or colleagues are not always malicious; sometimes they can add to self-knowledge. For instance, it may not always be self-apparent if one is arrogant or inconsiderate but behaviour can and does reveal our unconscious attitudes.
- It is often possible to trace back to the first time a fear or habit or attitude started because there is likely to be an emotional link that can act like a bloodhound tracking a scented object. There is no doubt that words have the power to awaken feelings. Popular songs immediately come to mind in this respect. One client was really upset and made to feel guilty over being wrongly accused of theft at work. His highly stressed condition seemed entirely out of proportion. He was sleepless and constantly angry. It turned out that many years earlier he had been humiliated and socially ostracised when held under suspicion because something was missing at school. He had managed to repress those unjustified guilt feelings for many years until they were revived when he was wrongly accused again, causing an explosive emotional reaction.
- The self-revealing aspect of this episode was realising why he had reacted so angrily with a sense of injustice in various situations. It provided him with evidence and insight into the way emotions can forge a link between present and past and how repressed feelings can lie at the root of exaggerated reactions.

The methods recommended and used by Freud and Jung – free association and dream association, to probe the unconscious mind as a means of uncovering tensions existing between the civilised and uncivilised self – have already been referred to. One of the main difficulties to be overcome when these methods are used in self-help psychotherapy is *resistance,* especially in relation to free association, dream interpretation and meditational analysis. Resistance can take the form of:

    a) Changing the subject on which you are concentrating,
    b) Pretended indifference,
    c) Breaking off treatment or
    d) Reluctance to start in the first place through fear of unearthing painful memories and feelings.

But one advantage of being your own therapist is that if you do weaken in your efforts to understand yourself, you can always buck up courage to tackle your problems again at any time without having to search for another therapist.

You can pre-empt resistance to a certain extent through hinting at the things you secretly dread; posing such questions as:
    What was the worst thing that ever happened to me?
    What was the worst thing I ever did or said?
    Did I ever feel terribly guilty about anything?

- This method could be likened to a laser being aimed directly at its target, as in a medical situation. The three questions given above may save beating about the bush and spending time

on secondary aspects. A psychotherapist might be wary of causing too much distress to a client with such direct questions, preferring to ease things out gradually; but if you are your own therapist and you are asking yourself a sensitive, leading question, then you are in control – no one is pressuring you to do anything.
- Patiently coercing your memory bank to reveal buried thoughts and feelings can be like trying to open an obstinate mussel or clam: you may need to doggedly persist several times. The more painful the memory the more you are likely to encounter distractions and misleading signposts, but with practice your concentration should improve.

Pre-retirement, I would sometimes say to a client: 'See if you have the courage to talk about the thing you really don't want to talk about'. Sometimes it would work straightaway; occasionally in a later session. Through self help psychotherapy you could use other means:-

- Another way of uncovering repressed memories is by getting a trusted friend to ask penetrating questions such as those posed above.
- If this method is not practicable, write down all the things you don't want to admit to yourself or to anyone. Nobody else need ever see it but you might at least bring to the surface thoughts and feelings that have smouldered in your unconscious for years. An example of this is the retention of guilt feelings. If only the two sisters who are featured in the following situation had been persuaded by a trusted friend to seek psychological help

much earlier than they did, they could have saved themselves many years of confusion and domestic conflict due to the fact that their husbands could not understand why they did not welcome physical contact.

The two sisters had carried a burden of shame and guilt from childhood into their early twenties because their father, a sexual abuser, had led them to believe that what they had done was normal and natural. As the sisters got older they blamed themselves and could not discuss their awful experience with anyone because of this.

Eventually, life became so difficult that they reluctantly agreed to take part in a television programme in the hope that it would release them from the stress of maintaining the secret that had already driven one of them to alcohol addiction, which had led to a car accident. Quite clearly 15 or more years of festering guilt and domestic conflict could not go on, and one thing that spurred them into bringing things into the open was a desire to encourage hundreds of people who were also tortured by guilt through no fault of their own, to save themselves years of unnecessary self recrimination and anguish by summoning enough courage to get psychological assistance without delay.

CONFIDENCE

Confidence can, to a certain extent, be acquired through education, achievement and wealth. But in order for it to be truly rooted and not feigned, common aspects of confidence such as self-esteem, assertiveness and optimism should ideally be embedded in the mind and emotions by means of loving care before many steps have been taken along the yellow brick road.

Unfortunately, a large number of people have not received enough love, care and encouragement during their early years when basic attitudes tend to be formed; or their confidence might have been shattered by too much criticism; by being regarded with less favour than another sibling, or due to lack of affection from parents who were too emotionally immature to express love or too lacking in psychological insight to give praise.

The *rejection* syndrome, which lies behind many a person's lack of confidence, can be experienced in many ways; not everyone, for instance, takes to boarding school at an early age. Looking at it from a child's point of view, it is not difficult to see why being sent away from those you love and need may be seen as rejection, no matter what reason or excuse parents may give.

Ignoring or shouting at a child who looks to you for affection and encouragement can obviously be very damaging to that child's self-esteem, confidence and view of the world, but busy, overwrought parents with no training in child care and very little self-awareness are often responsible for this type of behaviour as they try to cope with their most important and difficult task.

Alcohol and confidence

People can improve self-confidence more effectively through psychological insight than by entering the illusory world of the alcoholic in search of what is commonly known as Dutch courage. But advertisements are still allowed to give young people the impression that it is acceptable and adult to drink alcohol, without the type of warnings imposed on the sale of tobacco. And the negative and damaging effects that alcohol can have – costing thousands of lives every year, and causing the break-up of innumerable families – is given little or no attention. It is commonly known that too much alcohol can seriously affect a person's ability to cope with life. But how much is too much?

Researchers from Wellesley College in Massachusetts, USA have concluded, with the help of brain scans, that even seven pints of beer (or the equivalent) each week can shrink the brain. Heavy drinkers' brains were seen to be 1.6 per cent smaller than the brains of teetotallers. Teenagers, in particular, may need to be informed more often that *dangerous amounts* are much smaller than had previously been supposed, and that although in the short term, alcohol may appear to bolster confidence, they risk becoming dependent on a habit that claims a large number of lives each year.

Confidence is obviously badly affected when alcohol is taken to such excess that it lowers a person's likeability, capability and self esteem. Many teenagers have criminal records because of alcohol-induced behaviour, yet information regarding damaging social habits is conspicuous by its absence in the average school curriculum.

Dale Carnegie wrote a hugely popular book called *How to Win Friends and Influence People*, which has sold millions of copies and is continuously in print throughout Britain and the United States. He knew quite a lot about the power of words because he used to lecture business people on self-assertion and achieved international recognition through public speaking courses, which still bear his name to this day.

The power of words to influence behaviour should not be underestimated. Words can, after all, inspire confidence and courage. And if encouraging words don't come from someone else, they can come from *you* in the form of positive auto-suggestions. An important point about repeated auto-suggestion is that, as advertisers and politicians have found, repetition tends to impress things on the mind.

Teachers still use the repetition technique when helping children to learn multiplication tables. And plenty of people have gained courage for various challenges and situations by repeating, in thought or spoken word, the type of slogan shown below, which serves to increase confidence:-

Auto-suggestions are likely to be even more effective in enabling you to achieve objectives if they are backed up by greater efforts to be socially acceptable. Confidence in the art of conversation can be acquired through experience. Talking with comparative strangers is much easier if you think you are likeable, so why not convince yourself that you really are likeable by repeating on suitable occasions the following mantra:-

I am likeable

I am lovable

I am capable

C I A

The abbreviation CIA, standing for 'courage, insight and action', is easy to understand, though not always easy to put into action; but when it is resolutely applied, all kinds of problems can be satisfactorily resolved, whether they are of a practical, emotional or psychological nature. The formula is abbreviated as follows:

Courage is **C**
(Psychological and emotional) Insight is **I**
Action is **A**

CIA provides a systematic approach to problems experienced by the majority of people. Although the system is simple, it can be a potent recipe for change.

Courage is required if we are to face up to a problem instead of shelving it or refusing to admit its existence - as in many cases of harmful addictions.

Insight: There is a distinction between intellectual insight and emotional insight: the former may be a subconscious defence mechanism used to prevent progress to deeper and less pleasant levels of awareness; but emotional insight is believed to be essential for effective treatment of social and psychological problems.

Action can of course be on several different levels: mental, emotional, physical, moral and social. When insight and action help a self-centred person to be more sociable and at ease, with greater understanding and tolerance of other people's feelings, it reveals a spiritual aspect of psychological insight. It also shows that when the three aspects of CIA interact, fundamental changes can occur almost magically. For instance, when we lose a fear of failure it becomes possible to *do and dare* as never before in social life and at work, and as we gain confidence we are more likely to value and accept ourselves for what we are, with no need to pretend and no need to prove anything to anyone.

THE BURDEN OF HABITUAL PRETENCE

The American songwriter Irving Berlin poetically described pretence as 'putting on the Ritz'. Most of us resort to this on occasions, but pretentiousness on a continuous level seldom fools perceptive friends or colleagues; it can reveal a lack of confidence or insecurity commonly associated with boasting or excessive amounts of make-up.

But when CIA manages to turn pessimism into optimism, despair into hope, or pretentiousness into self-belief, a person's life can be said to have undergone a radical change for the better, with self criticism being replaced by the philosophy *I have my own qualities and values, I don't need to pretend to anyone about anything*. Newfound confidence arising from this sort of attitude could be likened to a car without grit in its carburettor - running free of brake trouble and with a clear window that gives wider vision.

Anyone who wonders whether they might appear to be pretentious could advisably take note of other people's comments and reactions. Prior to retirement as a psychotherapist, I encountered people who seemed mystified by their inability to form lasting relationships. I was moved on more than one occasion to enquire whether they could recall any criticism their former partners had made - adding that criticism can be enlightening.

THE ZONES OF EXPERIENCE

It is hoped that the following stages of emotional and psychological development will make it easier to assess progress. If you were fortunate enough to have had a secure and loving childhood with wise parents, progress from one zone to another might not have been too difficult; but if you were not so lucky, your journey along the testing yellow brick road could be hampered considerably, as the following indicators show. See if you can ascertain the zone most appropriate to your current situation:

The **Red** Zone is characterised by confusion and discontent. In order to escape to the Amber Zone, a realisation of what is wrong and a strong resolve to put things right is necessary.

The **Amber** Zone awaits those who have the necessary realisation of what their problem is, and a resolute *intention* to do something about it. However, intention alone is not enough. People who lack the courage to act on their intentions run the risk of being emotionally amberised, rather like fossilised insects trapped in the hard translucent amber of coniferous trees. But by proper actions you can escape from the Amber Zone.

The **Green Zone** is the Zone of positive action; people with a socially acceptable standard of morality, a compatible partner and a fulfilling job tend to stay longer in this zone. A function of CIA is to make the Green Zone more accessible to those who would normally find it difficult to cope when faced with conflict, confusion and discontent.

THE RED ZONE

(The Zone of Confusion and Discontent)

COMMON CAUSES OF DISCONTENT IN THE RED ZONE

Many problems that cause discontent and ruin relationships last a long time because of apathy and lack of self-knowledge, but by applying CIA and the self-conditioning technique described in this book, it is possible to do something about troublesome circumstances and personal characteristics contained in the list below that may be marring happiness, or frustrating ambitions:

1. A domestic power struggle.
2. Debt burdens and financial ineptitude.
3. Pretentiousness - due to low self esteem.
4. Ingrained pessimism.
5. Lack of purpose.
6. Loneliness - communication problems.
7. Too much work and no play.
8. Social timidity.
9. Self-destructive addictions.
10. An unbalanced lifestyle.
11. Unreasonable envy or jealousy.
12. Being too far removed from nature.
13. Being unfulfilled - due to a need of further education and training.

14   Laziness - due to fear of failure.
15   Boredom at work.
16   Unresolved psychological problems

Some of these matters are also referred to in other self analytical lists because they apply to various situations. There is space on the next page for making relevant notes.

TACKLING A CAUSE OF DISCONTENT
(Examples)

Cause of discontent

1. Domestic power struggle

2. Lack of purpose

Remedial action

1. Acceptance by both parties that there could be an emotional basis behind an urge to exercise power and always have your own way
Discuss; or get professional help.

2. **Make** a purpose: get new hobbies
Become less self-centred
Go for new experiences

IS FEAR KEEPING YOU IN THE RED ZONE?

Reasonable fears help us to survive but millions of people, regardless of talent and intelligence, are unnecessarily tormented by conditions such as:

1. Fear of failure or rejection.
2. Fear of responsibilities.
3. Fear of emotional commitment.
4. Fear of criticism or ridicule.
5. Fear of being unfavourably compared with others, including siblings.
6. Fear of not living up to expectations.
7. Fear of breaking away from religious conditioning.
8. Fear of being socially unacceptable.
9. Fear of change or challenges.
10. Fear of taking even well-considered risks.

Unless these sorts of situations are analysed and acted upon, they might lessen hope and lower self-esteem. Having specified unreasonable fears and anxieties that make you less of a person than you could be, *insight and action* should enable you to cope more effectively as you progress through a study of this book. Sometimes, straightforward practical steps are sufficiently effective, for example:

Fear of failure: Take on more testing responsibilities.
Fear of rejections: Accept rejection as a fact of life. Stop being a coward; risk disappointments.
Fear of taking a chance: Acknowledge that you can't afford a life of timidity, always avoiding risks: that would surely be too boring.

Auto-suggestions, backed up by relevant imagery, can increase confidence and self-belief. Start off a bold intention, using as few words as possible, with resolve and feeling:

> **I will………..**
> **I shall……..**
> **I can**
> **I am………**

FEAR OF TAKING A RISK

Politicians do not often sparkle with flashes of psychological insight into emotive and abstract issues but in 2004 the British Shadow Chancellor Oliver Letwin highlighted the need for a positive attitude toward 'risk' in public affairs. He said:

'The call to minimise risk is a call to minimise love, trust, hope, enterprise, compassion and courage; it is a call for a cowardly society.

Courage and cowardice are undoubtedly contentious, emotive subjects. During the First World War, soldiers, some still in their teens or early twenties, were put before a firing squad because of alleged cowardice. Psychological, emotional and neurological factors were not taken into consideration; but in the Second World War General Patton, the blood and guts American hero, was forced to make a public apology to the shell-shocked soldier he had publicly insulted by insinuation of cowardice.

The order for him to apologise was, in effect, an official recognition that there is more to courage and cowardice than meets the eye. Physical, mental and moral courage warrant analysis just as much as the fear complex. For example, courage can be linked to emotional maturity, genetic influence, motivation, values and conditioning: members of the armed forces are conditioned to endure and to risk danger and death through discipline, pride, duty and a common cause: whatever that may be. It is within parameters such as these that courage or cowardice can reasonably be assessed.

In this respect, geneticists could point to the as yet unquantifiable influence that genes can have on feelings and character. We know from our observation of animals that their instinct of aggression is inherited more strongly in some than in others. In humans it is likewise variable, depending, possibly, as much on genetic propensities, as on intellectual, moral and social issues.

The caution and timidity to which Oliver Letwin referred can be countered to some extent by Victorian parental standards based on self-discipline, personal pride, determination and endurance; but schools should surely share the additional responsibility of shaping the nation's character by encouraging positive attitudes, confidence and civilised values.

In the opinion of Jeffrey Caine, author of *The Constant Gardener*:

'The single most important thing in life is to find a person with whom you can share your life intimately. If you find love, you have found the greatest prize there is.'

Few would disagree with Jeffrey Caine's statement, though not every risk-taker is fortunate first time round. However, the saying *He who dares wins* has an element of truth, because everyone who dares to take a reasonable chance on a meaningful relationship has won a fight against fear of rejection or disappointment.

Many individuals probably know someone who is unhappy or lonely because they are too self-centred or because they lack the courage to risk sharing their life with another human being. This book is dedicated partially to helping those who need to understand the nature of fears and inhibitions that have prevented them from finding a person with whom they can share their life, if indeed that is what they truly desire.

DEALING WITH UNREASONABLE FEARS
(A case history)

Miss C's repressed fear was not serious enough to land her in the Red Zone, but she was annoyed and ashamed of her childish reaction to thunderstorms.

'I'm 23, and I feel really afraid of thunderstorms,' she said. 'I know it's silly, but I can't stop myself from panicking and diving under the table.'

As small children, we are of course inclined to *feel* rather than reason. Her mother's fearful example probably caused Miss C to register a similarly emotional response to thunderstorms, causing emotion to triumph over reason.

Could Miss C have released herself from this fear by means of DIY psychotherapy? Possibly, if she had visualised her mother scampering under the table. But her childhood memory had been suppressed – bottled up, because it was apparently too unpleasant to remember.

THE AMBER ZONE

(The Zone of Realisation and Intent)

CHEKHOV'S *THREE SISTERS* IN THE AMBER ZONE

Action is vitally important if the Green Zone is ever to be reached. In his play *Three Sisters*, Anton Chekhov, the famous Russian dramatist, exemplifies a situation involving three sisters who are perennially stuck in the Amber Zone. They spend many a dreary winter planning their departure from a dull, dispiriting, uninspiring village. Moscow, they believe, will be a place of adventure and romance, but their courage and resolve are not strong enough. They never do get to the Green Zone because they do not activate their realisations and intentions.

Urgent activation of realisation and intent could be considered necessary in cases such as these:

>Unreasonable jealousy
>Constant, irrational anger
>Psychological depression
>Unhappy relationships
>Frustrating, boring employment
>A feeling of being unworthy
>Loneliness

By using the CIA formula referred to frequently in this book, some of the above conditions could probably be eased or cleared up, though loneliness is not the easiest of problems to overcome without professional help if a person has emotional barriers to commitment and responsibilities.

LONELINESS

The friendless state, associated with unpopularity, implies a separation from other people's company. But who is generally responsible for this almost unbearable condition? The answer to that question is far from easy because there are so many reasons why a section of the world's population feels isolated. A number of examples are scattered throughout this book, but some causes are fairly common.

People with low self-esteem are sometimes under the impression that nobody would really like to know them. There could be several reasons for this:

Perhaps no one ever made them feel valued and loved.
If your parents find difficulty in showing affection, it is understandable if you avoid social occasions that might result in further rejection of your affections.

Sometimes even caring parents are unable or unwilling to disguise their preference for one child over another, causing feelings of jealousy and anger: as illustrated by the biblical story of Jacob, Joseph and the Coat of Many Colours.
Fear of rejection is one of the commonest causes of social

estrangement and is often fostered by guilt-laden low self-esteem. When guilt exists it may be because anger against a parent or sibling can make people feel unworthy.

Comedians may joke about Catholic guilt but it was no joke to thousands of those who had the religion imposed on them before they reached the age of reason and were too young to understand what was being done to their way of thinking and their right to lead their own life.

It is well known that the Catholic Church has in some countries an unwholesome attitude towards sex, tinting it, by implication, with guilt and a medieval allusion to sin. Sexual-related guilt has, judging by the high percentage of Catholics I have interviewed over many years, caused innumerable social and emotional problems, putting unnecessary difficulties in the way of their need to feel more likeable and more lovable

It is important for lonely people to come to the realisation that in the majority of cases, the rejecting is not being done by others, but by *themselves*: through fear, perhaps, of being emotionally hurt if their suppressed emotions are taken out of cold storage.

Several steps can be taken to avoid social isolation, apart from moving to a more inhabited area:-

1. Dare to participate in activities that can give you a socially useful experience.
2. With the aid of CIA, try to pinpoint the reason why (as shown by your behaviour) you are wary or afraid of emotional evolvement.
3. Specify, if possible, through meditation and dream

association, any specific incident or circumstance that coincides with the onset of what might be described as 'people phobia' and whether it relates only to the opposite sex.
4. Use CIA and auto-suggestion as a means of overcoming social timidity.
5. Visualise yourself going out more often and talking to people.
6. Interrupt self-centred thoughts by thinking about other people and other things.
7. By repeating the auto-suggestion 'I am likeable, I am lovable, I am capable', you may be able to raise self-esteem and make a fairer appraisal of your true worth.
8. If your parents were not capable of showing affection, make an effort to accept that they have probably loved you as far as they were able to love.
9. If you have been given the impression that you are no good and will never amount to anything, do not be unduly dismayed. History has shown that many famous and highly successful people received the same misguided treatment from parents or teachers who lacked the insight and the character to give a worthwhile opinion on qualities of character and potentialities.
10. Make a list of your good points: you may be more generous, more considerate, more forgiving, more understanding and more caring than many other people.
11. Take note of the fact that science has categorised you as a unique individual; not the same as either of your parents. This means that any regrettable

happening that may have occurred in their marriage doesn't have to happen in yours.

Furthermore, your future partner will not be a replica of either parent unless you subconsciously choose someone with identical characteristics, as sometimes happens when a person fails to mature through an important phase of emotional development. This type of situation sometimes elicits the remark: 'He married someone just like his mother'. But pre-armed and forewarned, you can determine to learn from your parent's experiences. If they were unsociable, for example, you could try to understand why; thereby increasing your emotional intelligence.

Aspects of loneliness – *individuality, independence and social isolation*

The urge to be sociable, a feature of the herd Instinct, appears to be on the wane except in third world countries where people are economically not so well contained and communities are still strengthened by close knit family units and a culture characterised by the sort of interdependence that once existed in the West. But the West now tends to be affected or afflicted by individuality, self-sufficiency and a watering down of social activities.

Geneticists have so far failed to detect an 'unsocial' gene, yet according to an estimate, by 2010 there will be about 31 million single households in the United States. A 2006 study published in the American Sociological Review stated that on average, Americans had only two close friends to confide in. Twenty-five per cent admitted they had no one in whom they could confide. Tragically, the United Kingdom situation appears to be proportionately similar. In England, doctors were once unpaid social workers but nowadays the time allowed for each patient, generally speaking, is three to five minutes.

The need to belong was poignantly expressed by a black and white cat with huge appealing eyes at a Blue Cross cattery for strays. My wife and I could not leave without him. It took more than a year of proffered affection before we earned his trust. Billy, as he came to be known, was no different from innumerable people who have a history of rejection. He needed time for his fear of being let down again to subside. The separation anxiety caused by the betrayal of his previous owner was so great that even after six years, he still hides behind our sofa whenever the bell rings; presumably through fear of being taken away.

There is in this example a clear parallel with people's need for affection and sense of belonging. But fear of rejection in humans can at least be ameliorated by talk therapy provided the lonely person does not shy away and has the courage to go on a journey of self-discovery or can somehow be convinced of his/her self worth.

I warmed to the sound and the sight of a group of people animated by companionship. On enquiry, I discovered that their friendship arose from a common interest in tennis: though the buzz of their conversation covered a variety of topics. If hobbies were to be given adequate time and mention on the school curriculum, young people might be able to avoid a certain degree of loneliness in later life through the companionship and lasting interest that can be gained through literature, music, sport and other interests of a social nature. Our identity is, after all, determined largely by what we do and what we know. Many would agree that parents and education authorities have a duty to prepare children against the numbing spectre of loneliness by taking preventative measures at an early stage.

Happiness and Loneliness

The English philosopher Bertrand Russell wrote a book called the Conquest of Happiness. Many of the things he mentioned relate to the conquest of loneliness. He believed, as many do, that happy people are in harmony with themselves and that companionship and cooperation are essential elements in the happiness of the average person. Conversely, loneliness is often linked with the absence of inner harmony, as with 'identity' problems, and a feeling that one is an outsider.

Conscience, he maintained (as humanists do) is not bestowed or inflicted by any sort of god; it varies in different parts of the world and is connected with being in agreement with tribal custom. The practice of cannibalism is an example of this. Cannibals appear to have no conscience about eating members of their own species, it was, and perhaps still is, part of their tribal custom. In simple terms, conscience is , in civilised society, really a fear of being found out.

Russell stressed that happiness is largely determined by a person's outlook on life. In this respect it is worth mentioning once again that auto-suggestion can, through the impact of words and thoughts on emotions, help to change attitudes and outlook when used repetitively with imagination and when combined, if necessary, with remedial therapy.

The Conquest of loneliness

Effective measures for the conquest of loneliness include

a) The courage and humility to undergo a personal or professional assessment of your character, personality and mental outlook.
b) The courage to risk rejection and disappointment.
c) The imagination and determination to change your social attitude.

Loneliness and related depression can be overcome in some cases by situations and events that can *raise the spirit;* cheerful music, exercise and travel, optimistic and positive auto-suggestions i.e. 'Things can only get better. The best is yet to come'. Loneliness may be allayed by viewing a DVD of your favourite comedian, close and regular contact with animals and anything that helps to take your mind off yourself, such as being involved in an organisation which aims to help people who are in less fortunate circumstances.

Happy situations can be infectious. Comedian Ken Dodd (affectionately known as Doddy) must have helped many people forget their troubles by singing his trademark song: 'Happiness, happiness, the greatest thing that I possess, I thank the Lord that I am blessed with more than my share of happiness'. He sang this song while things were going badly wrong. He had just had his wallet lightened by gentlemen from the Inland Revenue, but he put on a cheerful face and made fun of himself in order to make people forget their own problems. Perhaps more of us could take a tip from entertainers who ensure that no matter what happens, the show must go on.

Motivations

If your life is motivated by a need for respect and an inordinate yearning for success and financial security, to the detriment of intellect and widely acceptable values, you could benefit by realising what sort of security you are after, because to spend one's life and energy chasing money and wealth can so easily be an overcompensation for lack of emotional security or a distraction from emotional commitment. This may mean, if your life seems empty, that no amount of wealth or power could bring you what you may desire most of all, a release from loneliness.

A few minutes each day away from the rush and the roar might be enough to transform the life of anyone who, on reflection, decides that things have got to change for the better. Charles Dickens, that master of characterisation, put in a good word for the trivialities of life when he created the trivialities connected with Christmas. In his novel *A Christmas Carol*, Scrooge's life was motivated, as many of us know, by a need for financial security above all else; but through Dickens he was transformed when he moved away from *self*. The great writer may have seen the best of times, but it was the worst of times that enabled him to show the uneasy relationship between motivations, morals and values.

FRIENDSHIPS: IN THE GIVE AND TAKE OF LIFE

Whether we like it or not, society works on a give and take principle. If you want to run a successful business you have to supply what people need or want, otherwise your product or service will not be deemed acceptable or worthy.

The same applies in human relationships. A friend in need may be regarded as an untimely nuisance, but if he or she has previously helped or encouraged you when you were in need, you are more likely to return an act of kindness.

It has to be acknowledged that some of us are not naturally altruistic. In a survival-minded world, the selfish motive is like an inflated ball floating on water; it keeps on coming to the surface no matter how many times you push it down.

Even a mother-child relationship is not always altruistic. If the mother, through no fault of her own, is unable to show love, the child, who has not experienced her love, may not be willing or able to respond with demonstrable affection; unless, as years go by, time, that great healer, extends an empathetic hand.

Your efforts to get a friend by being a friend may depend on you becoming courageously venturesome. If you are prepared to risk disappointment or rejection, challenge yourself to do so; picture opening up a conversation with a stranger. The following auto-suggestion could put you in the right frame of mind.

IT'S GETTING EASIER AND MORE ENJOYABLE TO TALK TO PEOPLE.

By making a note of the number of social contacts you make each week, you should manage to assess whether your social activities have increased.

AWARENESS IN THE AMBER ZONE

Gaining an awareness of our faults and inclinations can appear as difficult as ever, despite the efforts of Sigmund Freud, novelists and poets. Robert Burns had a wise head but even he realised how difficult it can be to see ourselves as others see us. He once pensively declared:

> 'O wad some power
> the giftie gie us
> to see oursels
> as others see us'.

Since the poet died, psychoanalysis has made important inroads into self-knowledge but one of the main obstacles to psychological insight that still remains is the power of emotions to assist us in self-deception. So we owe it to ourselves to try to recognise characteristics that may necessitate remedial action, for example:

a) Being a taker - not a giver
b) Lacking in kindness and consideration.
c) Being boastful and bullying
d) Being too critical - not encouraging
e) Being unsociable
f) Being too self-centred
g) Being afraid to risk failure

h) Being afraid to show affection
i) Having excessive reactions to criticism
j) Being lazy and indecisive due to lack of self-belief
k) Lacking emotional control

By going through the above list with someone who knows you well, you may be less inclined to gloss over unflattering characteristics: (a or f, perhaps).

But we should not be too disheartened over imperfections; life is, after all, a learning experience, and it takes most of us a whole lifetime to mature emotionally and morally.

Notes

Intentions and Determinations

For consideration	For action

SELF-ANALYSIS THROUGH SELF AWARENESS

As Robert Burns fully realised, to be aware of our own good or bad characteristics is difficult because we usually see what we want to see. But it is possible to come to a fairly accurate assessment of weaknesses and strengths through a retrospective scan of deeds or actions performed in the previous month or two. As a wise man once said:

By their works ye shall know them.

It could prove worthwhile getting an honest assessment of one's likeability from a friend who, hopefully, will be honest enough to point out things that might otherwise be glossed over when compiling a personal questionnaire on matters such as:

1. What should I do in order to merit an ideal partner?
2. Am I too selfish to love wholeheartedly?
3. What is top of my list of priorities? Do I need to change that list?
4. Which criticism from friends and colleagues has

caused surprise?
5. Would I buy a second-hand car from somebody like myself?

As far as awareness is concerned, we cannot be conscious of anything unless it has been registered in the mind through memory, emotions or the senses, therefore *experience*s (vehicles of the senses) are essential to anyone who wishes to live a full life.

Stimulating and challenging experiences

If we deny ourselves and our children stimulating and challenging experiences, we thereby limit awareness, and opportunities for fun, adventure and much of what might have been known, valued and contributed during the brief period of consciousness known to the human species as life.

The auto-suggestion on the next page could prove very helpful to people in need of confidence and courage.

A quaint Victorian saying:
 'If things don't alter they'll remain as they are'.

For those who are too cautious or afraid to take on new responsibilities, the following auto-suggestion should ideally be combined with an appropriate mental picture of a particular happening, and with a feeling of determination.

I have the courage to risk rejection or failure

A few mental repetitions prior to sleep could, if persisted in over a suitable period, prove very effective.

THE GREEN ZONE

(The zone of positive action)

EMOTIONAL INTELLIGENCE

Entry into the Green Zone becomes a credible reality when obstructive mental conflicts and unreasonable fears have been largely resolved. In some cases, very ordinary and logical action can merit entry into that zone, such as getting out of debt, changing your job, or acquiring a home of your own; but having reached the zone of positive actions, *emotional intelligence* may still remain a necessity for people who wish to consolidate their Green Zone status because there is a constant need to be aware of reactions and impulses. Emotions play a far greater role in thought, decision-making and individual success than is sometimes realised.

Quiet meditation and an imaginary rehearsal before an event can be of considerable help during preparation for demanding situations. Counting up to ten before giving way to an annoying impulse is also a proved and effective method of self-control. If, for instance, you wish to avoid the annoying habit of interrupting people when they are talking, you can, by pausing a few seconds, check yourself; and maybe come to the realisation that for some reason or other you could be an attention-seeker. This in itself may raise your awareness of the need and nature of emotional intelligence.

By making a note of any irrational behaviour displayed over several weeks, it should be possible to avoid or cut down the number of times that emotion overcomes reason; acknowledging, of course, that occasionally, emotional decisions and actions are unreasonably right (falling in love could be cited as an example).

PART TWO

(Action through thought control)

ACTION THROUGH THOUGHT CONTROL

It is not possible to think of more than one thing at a time, so you can try to ensure that only positive thoughts shall be allowed to affect your attitudes and actions. But if, during an unguarded moment, a negative thought does slip through, such as 'I don't think I've got much of a chance', that negative thought can be pushed out of the way with a defiant feeling of determination, as you think:

'I'll be relaxed and positive.'

If you are about to turn down a promising opportunity due to lack of confidence, affirm several times with emotion and conviction:

'Nothing ventured, nothing gained. I have the courage to accept responsibilities'.

If your spirits are down after a serious setback, repeat a confidence-boosting thought:-

'The best is yet to come. I welcome a challenge.'

Stiffen your resolve to take on a new task with an assertive sentence beginning with:

'I can and I will…'

FEELING SOCIALLY AT-EASE

Human destiny has been affected largely by people who, in moments of solitude, invented, schemed and created with feeling, *imagination* and self-belief. When these qualities are combined with related auto-suggestions, even day-to-day situations can be more effectively tackled. For example, if you avoid social events because they make you feel self-conscious or uncomfortable, just relax in a quiet place and imagine yourself enjoying a conversation with complete strangers, as you repeat in your mind:

'Talking to people is becoming more enjoyable.'

By audaciously confronting anxieties, you could incidentally be successful in overcoming an irrational fear of being looked at or spoken about; especially if you remind yourself, prior to a social event, that most people are far too wrapped up in their own affairs to be thinking about you, and that it is usually self-centred individuals with an exaggerated impression of their own importance who fool themselves into believing that people are talking about them.

But a consistent fear that people might be unfriendly may be due to your own repressed hostility toward them. A limited degree of paranoia is fairly common but psychological insight could, in some cases, help people to recognise the source and nature of their unsocial behaviour; if not, individual therapy may be needed.

When choreographers compose a sequence of steps and moves for a dance, they tend to use mental pictures. You too can picture yourself coping with a situation as you apply relevant auto-suggestions that are reasonable, brief and repeated, such as:

I am likeable
I am lovable
I am capable

Daily repetitions need not take more than a minute over an appropriate number of weeks. In this way it becomes possible to create a more positive image of yourself as you mentally and positively accentuate acceptable aspects of the person you desire and intend to acquire.

(Case history)

A shy guitarist used to break into a nervous sweat whenever he had to face an audience until, during the course of hypnotherapy, he was able to uncover a childhood memory of being urged to recite a poem in front of his parent's friends.

He was asked to imagine himself playing confidently in front of a large audience, concentrating fully on giving people enjoyable entertainment. After an apparently successful session, the relieved guitarist was assured that the childhood memory would never bother him again.

Similar improvements can be brought about by self-analysis coupled with suitable suggestions and related mental images. The key to success, as already mentioned, can often be a revealing link-up of past and present emotional situations.

ACTING RESPONSIBLY

One of the best ways to be a worthy member of the Green Zone is to act responsibly in a positive manner, even taking on tasks that contain the possibility of failure.

In business and politics an acceptance of responsibility is of course essential to success. It certainly was to Winston Churchill. He was not a great success at school, and lived under the shadow of famous ancestors. How did he manage, with such a burden of expectations, to prove himself? His answer was to be a bold, active and confident risk-taker. He knew that experiences can provide knowledge: knowledge of what we are and what we are capable of. As for risk-taking: Winston had this to say:

'Success is going from failure to failure with no loss of enthusiasm'.

To him, responsibility was the spice of life. There's a lot to say for that type of attitude: if we are afraid of responsibility we are afraid of life. Two of the most significant differences between children and adults are that:

a) Children rely on others to take responsibilities.
b) They expect or hope for instant satisfaction.

In both examples a state of emotional immaturity exists: whether in children or in adults who have the same dependant attitudes.

OUR ANIMAL HERITAGE

Charles Darwin referred to 'the awesome power of the Will'. When this power is expressed in relation to need and desire, it is a force to be reckoned with at a time in history when there are so many interesting opportunities and worthwhile aims to be considered and so many challenges that can strengthen and fulfil a person's needs, desires, intentions and hopes.

The combined potential of need, desire and will appears to have been used effectively by herds of elephants in Sri Lanka. When their survival was threatened by tusk-hunters, some herds appear to have activated a much needed gene mutation that caused their calves to be born without tusks – a possibility that could stretch the credulity of many people, yet Bryan Appleyard, a knowledgeable writer on such matters, keeps an open mind on what is possible. He had this to say:

> *'The pathways by which genes express themselves are fiendishly complex.'*

If elephants, through need, desire and will, really can exercise such powers, who can tell to what extent our ascendancy over other species might have been genetically furthered in this way?

We have much in common with elephants, walruses and many other animals, as well as domestic pets: a capacity for affection, desire, grief and anger; but in addition to these similarities there is visual memory, a capacity which appears to be closely linked to development of the brain.

A komodo dragon gave a demonstration of its capacity to visualise when film star Sharon Stone and her then husband Phil Bronstein saw it at a private zoo in Los Angeles. During their visit, Phil unwisely accepted the zoo-keeper's invitation to join him in the dragon's cage, but was advised to remove his white tennis shoes in case the ten-foot Indonesian lizard mistook them for its favourite delicacy - white rats. But Bronstein's precaution of removing his white shoes did not deter the dragon from clamping onto his feet, (which were also white) until its mouth was forced open. As could be expected, Bronstein needed lengthy medical attention after that encounter, which apparently proved the dragon's ability to remember, however vaguely, the shape and colour of white rats.

This in itself may not seem very remarkable, but it does appear to show that visual memory might have been an important supplement to the basic instincts of that particular species.

The inherited powers previously mentioned might indeed have had some bearing on the birth of tusk-free Sri Lanka elephant calves; in recent times there has been growing awareness of the power of mind and feelings over the body.

An example of this came from a resourceful surgeon in Texas, USA, who gave some of his patients, who were suffering from painful arthritis in their knees, a fake operation. Seven years later, they allegedly remained cured. Similar methods have reportedly been shown to work for asthmatics, heart and cancer patients, and some with Parkinson's disease.

Professor Kathy Sykes, author of *Alternative Medicine*, who took a close look at the paranormal in a television documentary on the 'placebo' effect, in regard to medical experiments by the Texas surgeon, also examined faith-healing carried out by a charismatic preacher healer at a football stadium. It left her with a conviction that the placebo effect, which can give rise to *hope, expectation and reward*, could advantageously be used in cash-strapped areas of health services.

Some may consider that the above examples of mind over matter offer yet another reminder of the powers we can call upon to express ourselves mentally and imaginatively, as in cases of stigmata.

STIGMATA AND AUTO-SUGGESTION

Will, emotions, needful desire and visual imagery (all aspects of man's animal heritage) were expressed dramatically by a monk who was absorbed in meditation and prayer in 1224 A.D. The monk was Francis of Assisi. During, or shortly after, his intense concentration on Christ's crucifixion wounds, similar wounds appeared on his own hands, feet, and right side. Francis of Assisi, who was later to found the Franciscan Order, was the first of many who afterwards replicated on themselves the wounds inflicted on Jesus Christ: a phenomenon known as 'stigmata'.

Some may choose to believe that this strange happening, so alien to our scientific age, has deep religious significance, but the consensus of medical and scientific opinion indicates that stigmatic personalities, invariably highly sensitive, stressed-up individuals, identify themselves so emotionally and imaginatively with the crucified Christ that they unwittingly 'suggest' the wounds upon themselves.

Fred Harrison, in his book *Stigmata*, gives details of an experiment by a German medic, Dr Alfred Lechler, in 1928. One of the doctor's patients, Elizabeth, was highly suggestible and prone to take upon herself many medical symptoms. She agreed to take part in an experiment proposed by Lechler; his objective being to prove that stigmata wounds can be induced in some people through hypnotic suggestions.

While she was in a hypnotised state, he asked her to concentrate on nails being driven into her hands and feet. The following day Elizabeth, who had no conscious memory of the event, was distressed to find that she did indeed bear the wounds of crucifixion on her hands and feet. Dr Lechler then assured her that the wounds would heal: and they did. Emboldened by his success, he then persuaded her to agree, during waking consciousness, to visualise tears of blood, such as she had seen in a photograph of the stigmatic Theresa Neuman, and to keep thinking of those images, imagining and feeling they were happening to her. In a matter of hours, blood was allegedly seen to come from inside her eyelids and flowed down her cheeks. Lechler then told her that the tears would stop immediately - and they did.

Even the Catholic Church has treated stigmatism with caution and scepticism, having assumed that stigmatic wounds and bleeding might have been of a psychosomatic nature.

It is reasonable to conclude that intense concentration, deep fervour, a vivid imagination and the power of subconsciously willing such a happening may, in highly sensitive people, enable their minds to activate bodily changes; though of course to a lesser degree than the limb replacements wrought by worms, salamanders and other creatures.

Hypnosis and Suggestion

Need, desire, imagination, will and suggestion were undoubtedly key factors in the event that made it possible for a world-famous composer to regain faith in his ability to be creative again.

Sergei Rachmaninov, the Russian composer and pianist, had the equivalent of an author's mental block. He could still play the piano brilliantly and could remember the theoretical niceties of harmony and counterpoint, but his creativity had dried up. In desperation, he turned to hypnotherapy. After several sessions of positive suggestion, confidence and creative fluency were restored to such an extent that he thrilled the music fraternity with a wonderful new piano concerto. In gratitude, he dedicated his concerto to the person who had assisted in his recovery.

Hypnotic suggestions are not usually effective if there is resistance but Rachmaninov was fully receptive to the suggestion that he would return to his brilliant best.

Prayer and Auto-suggestion

The Freedom from Religion Foundation in the USA held a rally during which a prominent placard was displayed. It read:

PRAYER IS TALKING TO YOURSELF

Most people appear to believe in a Divine Creator but for anybody who doesn't, then praying really can seem rather like talking to no one.

Gods and religions come and go: and the religion a person is likely to follow relates in most cases to their country of birth and what their parents believe, rather than on informed choice.

Geographical and cultural factors have predetermined the lives and beliefs of many millions of people, particularly those who were systematically conditioned from childhood by a fascistic regime in control of the media and empowered to prevent citizens from following their own convictions.

Prayer is generally considered to be a force for good and is commonly believed to get results, whether for the believer or the intended beneficiary. There could, arguably, be plenty of evidence to support the efficacy of prayer insofar as the things we believe, anticipate or concentrate on do sometimes come true. It is probably a helpful way of attuning the mind to whatever is desired or needed, though it should not of course replace the pursuit of insight or courageous endeavour.

But a sceptical person might dispute an assumption that divine intervention could have anything to do with favourable results arising from prayer, arguing that if you bet often enough on horses favoured to win, you will, on the law of averages, also sometimes get your desired result. In both cases, hopes are only occasionally fulfilled.

Willing something to happen can, it is believed, be effective on an earthly level when people transmit intensified thought-waves (as in healing) that are energised by feeling. During WW2, a number of psychics were persuaded to attempt to negatively influence the enemy's war effort in this way.

Is prayer similar to auto-suggestion? Yes, prayer is usually about hopes, ambitions, good health, moral strength, self-improvement and good intentions. So are some of the auto-suggestions on printed slogans contained in this book. A defining difference, however, is that prayer is directed outwardly towards a supposedly all powerful god, whereas auto-suggestions are directed to the power within, which enables us to help ourselves.

A crucial issue regarding the use of prayer appears to be whether you are spiritually dependent or whether you are spiritually self-contained. The situation could be applicable to a person's approach to adversity; if your transport breaks down in the middle of a desert, you can pray for help or you can roll up your sleeves and try to get it moving again. But in the normal course of events an inclination to rely on prayer need not deter anyone from taking advantage of the method for self-assertion and fulfilment known as auto-suggestion, because prayer itself can be regarded as a form of auto-suggestion, in that the person who is praying is mentally registering wishes, hopes or intentions; unwittingly implying to the subconscious mind that it is desirable for this or that to happen.

ACTION - DETERMINING FUTURE EVENTS

By using post-hypnotic suggestions - explained in part five (pages 234-5) - you can influence the way you are likely to react to an impending event: whether it involves a game of tennis or football, a scholastic examination, a social event, a business presentation, or calming your nerves during a driving test. By using a date or time or key word for an auto-suggestion to become effective, you may virtually pre-empt a situation – just like pressing a 'control' button. You can also use post-hypnotic suggestions to combat procrastination or finish a project. But, to reiterate: auto-suggestions should ideally be tailored realistically to what is possible and feasible in order to achieve the most favourable outcome.

Expectation, negative or positive, can play an important part in determining success or failure. Many city dwellers are probably familiar with the way they have preconditioned themselves subconsciously to step up or down an escalator even if it isn't moving; this shows the extent to which we can be affected by what we anticipate, whether in sport, exams or anything we are about to attempt. It also indicates the usefulness of *deliberately* raising expectancy when we are about to face a social situation or take part in a competitive event.

SHOULD WE FORCE-FEED ON NEW EXPERIENCES?

The answer to that question probably lies in another question: what happens if we are afraid to face challenges or new experiences? We will have only ourselves to blame if, after a boring, uneventful life we look back over the years with sadness and regret at the things we did not attempt to do because of laziness or fear of failure, instead of making things happen through courage, initiative and action.

In order to lead an interesting and purposeful life, we should be prepared to take a risk or two and philosophically learn from an occasional failure in any new experience we undertake.

It is said that we are what we *eat;* it is equally true to say that we are what we *experience,* for this largely determines the type of person who is likely to find us likeable or lovable, insofar as experiences have the effect of shaping character and personality.

Hans Christian Anderson, the author of memorable fairytales, typified those who have a thirst and a need for new experiences. At the tender age of fourteen, he left home alone and walked many miles with scant belongings; like a moth drawn to a candle he headed for the glittering city of Copenhagen. Once there, he plied his trade as a cobbler. In his spare time, the rustic youth with an uneducated accent scribbled fairytales that would entrance and charm adults and children throughout the world for many generations to come.

Hans had been reared in extremely disadvantaged circumstances both socially and financially, and probably did think he was socially unacceptable because of this. It has been suggested that one of his most successful stories, *The Ugly Duckling*, might have been centred on himself. Yet in spite of everything, the young writer had such strong self-belief that eventually he came to the attention of highly influential people when his first book of fairy stories was published in 1835, and was an honoured guest at the home of the internationally famous Charles Dickens.

New experiences that Hans ventured into certainly brought the esteem and recognition he had always needed, taking him from the degrading circumstances of his childhood in the Red Zone, to good fortune and social acceptance in the Green Zone

WAYS OF OVERCOMING EMOTIONAL STALEMATE

Information can change your life

If you are burdened with a mental block, unable to shake off inertia or indifference, you are in the Red Zone. But at least two practical steps can be taken:

1. Make a greater effort to socialise: people often give information about things in general that may in the course of conversation lead to insights and important experiences. For example, after nine lonely years, a person's life was changed when someone told her about the fan club of a famous singer she greatly admired. Since joining the club, she has made a number of friends; they travel to meetings, correspond, telephone and exchange records and articles about the admired personality. The lady's mantelpiece is no longer bare at Christmas: she has plenty of greetings cards from fellow music-lovers. An incidental reference to the club by an acquaintance had enriched her life considerably.

2. Seek out a location where there are trees, vegetation

and the sounds and smells of nature. Walk a lot more; the exercise releases happy hormones: and the stimulation might awaken hope, imagination, and dormant realisations.

3. A course of training of some sort might increase self-confidence and awareness, as might psychological help. You may gain knowledge and widen your experiences by attending evening classes. Daring to be socially more venturesome in a new setting may stimulate you emotionally, the way a fresh wind stirs a stalled sailing ship in a motionless sea.

The following poem by Robert Herrick might remind you how quickly time passes by:

> **Counsel to Girls**
> Gather ye rosebuds while ye may,
> Old time is still a-flying:
> And this same flower that smiles today,
> Tomorrow will be dying.

A warning to everyone that action may be necessary before it is too late to realise hopes and intentions. It may take a crisis to jerk oneself out of a rut but quite often new experiences can do the trick when they bring psychological and emotional insight. If you don't know why you've reached stalemate, you may find a clue by scanning through the following list:

Fear of emotional commitment

Lack of confidence
Fear of responsibility
Feelings of inferiority
Lack of imagination
Lack of incentive and loss of interest
No clear objective or goal
Limited experience of life
Laziness or pessimism
Priority of values in doubt
Parents' expectations too high
Absence of required skills
Social and emotional problems
Harmful addictions
Lack of moral courage

But take heart: many individuals have overcome such obstacles through the application of CIA. and/or a change of lifestyle. The sooner you can locate and gain insight into the cause or causes of your problem, the sooner you may be able to shake off mental and emotional lethargy.

Below are typical situations from the above list. With insight so far gained you may, by looking through it, locate a clue to your mental block.

Example 1 - *No clear objective or goal to aim for.* Aims and objectives usually involve responsibilities and effort. Take on new responsibilities.

Example 2 - *Lack of confidence.* Perhaps you have begun to lose faith in your ability. Acknowledge that where there's the will there's a way; that at some time or another everyone has to risk failure, or cease to progress. Being successful is easier once you have found something you enjoy doing; perhaps there is still time and opportunity to find an activity better suited to your talents or changed attitude to life.

Mental and Emotional Stimulation – A means of overcoming Stalemate.

Literature can stir curiosity, entertain, educate, and be such a valuable source of interest that any parents who fail to encourage their children to read may be guilty of stunting their intellectual development and could run the risk of unsettling the spirit of that icon of English literature, Jane Austen, who held the opinion that novels can express: *'the greatest power of the mind, the most thorough knowledge of human nature, the happiest delineations of its variations and the liveliest effusions of wit and humour'.*

In a world bedazzled by electronic information devices, literature containing the thoughts, the wisdom and the imagination of past generations is gathering dust in many public libraries. One reason for this could be the emergence of television, but an increasing number of parents find that they really are too busy or tired to find time to read to their children after a hard day's work: which is most regrettable when one considers that as children we are more receptive to emotional and mental stimulation than at any other time in life.

Social experiences can help to release emotional blocks.

The most obvious reason for force-feeding on new experiences is to avoid staying alone too much feeling sorry for yourself. Perhaps you lack confidence and feel isolated; however, you probably have a rough idea of the odds on making a friend if:

- a) You spend five evenings a week indoors, compared with:
- b) If you go out five evenings a week to increase your social activities.

PART THREE

(Psychological and Emotional Insight)

ASPECTS OF LOVE

The kindness factor

How can love exist if there is no kindness? In 1995 the United States Congress proclaimed a Random Acts of Kindness Week. Streetwise Congress members fully realised how important this particular virtue is to their nation's struggle against violence, prejudice and selfish behaviour.

Kindness wears several types of hat; in every stratum of society its related qualities of empathy, understanding and tolerance are to be found. Some people are kind because they feel it is a religious duty; some because they hope to qualify for imagined joys of an imagined paradise; and some because they are actively and humanely empathetic by nature.

The caretaker of a block of flats became aware that I was struggling to disconnect a washing machine. Although it was his day off, he straightaway started to help. This spontaneous gesture caused me to offer him payment, which he declined.

Later on I thought: 'I met a good man today: it was an uplifting experience.'

When an act of kindness is performed on impulse, it has a spiritual aspect: not necessarily associated with any religion or philosophy.

Eleanor Roosevelt believed that:
'when you cease to make a contribution you begin to die.'

Pliny the Elder said:
'It is godlike for mortals to assist others.'

Ralph Waldo Emerson expressed the view that
'one of the most beautiful compensations of life is that no man can sincerely try to help another without helping himself'.

When someone asked the Dalai Lama to define his religion, he replied:
'My religion is simple. My religion is kindness.'

Gloria Wade Gayles took a philosophical and psychological approach. She said:-
'Kindness is the only avenue toward a larger self.'

Jesus Christ, that well known philosopher, said the same thing in a different way:
'He that loseth himself shall find himself.'

A KIND OF LOVING

The sort of love situation we find ourselves in may be determined to some extent by luck, rash decisions, sexual attraction or faulty motivation.

A Case history

Mrs B, on the point of tears, said: 'Most of my friends think I've got a good marriage. My husband has a regular job: we have a son and a nice house.'

'So what's the trouble,' I asked. 'Is he an alcoholic?'

'Oh no,' she replied. 'He stays at home five evenings a week but just watches the telly till he falls asleep. At weekends he goes fishing with his pals. I've given up cooking him a Sunday dinner.'

'Do you love him?' I asked.

'Yes,' she said, after a pause.

'Is he kind?'

'What do you mean?' She asked, looking rather puzzled.

'Well, isn't he ever affectionate, considerate, or sensitive to your feelings and needs?'

'Oh no,' she said, lowering her gaze and moving her head sideways several times.

Further prompting revealed that her hasty marriage was

based almost entirely on physical attraction and a desire to break away from home.

Her marriage might have been saved through common interests and mutual respect, but she found herself living in an emotional vacuum, destined to join the ranks of separated couples who hope for better luck next time round.

Mrs B had become embittered and cynical because of her experiences, but the more insight she has gained from her hasty, ill-considered situation, the less she should need to depend on luck in any future partnership.

Hopefully, she will enrich her life, improve her conversational powers and acquire new interests, so that she does not depend entirely on anyone else for mental stimulation. She confessed to being too depressed to concern herself with other people for the time being and was, as the saying goes, 'stuck in the mud', unable to move.

It is not entirely true to say that we get what we deserve in life. Finding the right partner is obviously not always an easy or rational matter. Judging by divorce statistics in the western world, far too many of us should not be so careless and ill-prepared for one of the most significant commitments we are ever likely to make, especially if spiritual aspects are obscured by an emotional fog.

> SPIRIT: *A secular definition:* the non-physical part of a person, which is the seat of emotion and character.

Emotional rapport, character, humour, trust, mental rapport

and mutual respect are some of the more obvious aspects of lovability that should ideally attract us to each other.

Philosophers and psychologists may strive to define the magic and mystery of love but lyricists and poets are generally more successful in describing that sublime, unsettling state. In a heart-warming song from the perennial musical *Showboat,* the lyricist describes what love is without actually explaining it:

> 'I can't explain, it's surely not his brain that makes me thrill.
> I love him ... because he's just my Bill.'

The operas of Puccini owe their appeal largely to the recurrent theme of love: with all its bewilderment, wonder and pain; as do authors who keep romance alive by prolonging it with crafted misunderstandings before finally resolving disagreements and jealousies.

In Shakespeare's *A Midsummer Night's Dream*, love is administered via a magic potion that overcomes all reason. The late actress Bette Davis once made a remark that suggested she might have been fooled by some sort of love potion; she cynically viewed the sexual aspect of love as 'nature's chemical manipulation: nature's con to perpetuate the species'.

*

Romantic love is certainly not a simple matter. A well known song poses the question

> 'Why do I love you? Maybe it's because you love me.'

There may be some substance to this in cases where a

person is hopeful and flattered by someone's declaration of love and is thereby minded to yield to an emotional commitment that could be described as a kind of love.

*

A number of desirable compatibilities are likely to be undeveloped between two diverse, complicated partners, and it can take a lot of insight, tolerance, patience and compromise to smooth out the creases. Understanding, tolerance and patience could justifiably be classified as spiritual aspects of love.

Below is a summary of related differences and problems so far referred to:

Differences and Problems

Divisive situations can often be fairly easy to predict, unless looked at through rose-coloured spectacles. *Giver marries taker*, for instance, or when one partner's aim is financial security.

*

Obsessive preoccupation with work and career, which deprives partner and children of the care and companionship they deserve and, perhaps, the time and attention children usually associate with love.

*

If you allow yourself to be used as a doormat, you will lose self-respect and the respect of your partner.

*

Anti-parent feelings are sometimes transferred to one's partner. Be mindful and analytical about irrational, explosive reactions: they often have their roots in childhood frustrations that were never expressed. It is surely better to discover these things 'before' commitment, rather than afterwards .Couples who do not carry out intimate discussions at an early stage in their relationship are, generally speaking, more likely to suffer the consequences later on.

*

Mutual respect - a dangerously fragile sentiment, and one of love's less obvious splendours – is put at risk in countless relationships that have floundered on the supposedly harmless *affair* that shatters trust, even though 'it really didn't mean a thing, dear'.

*

Enduring love may depend on any of the following compatibilities:

A Honouring each other's individuality.
B Affection and generosity
C Sexual needs.
D Generosity of spirit
E Verbal and mental rapport; if this ceases to exist, what else is there?
F An equal partnership presupposes a degree of mutual dependence and independence, not unilateral control.
G Religious differences should ideally be sorted out prior to emotional and legal commitment; so should the vitally important issue of whether or not to have a family.
   Incredibly, these things are sometimes overlooked when people marry in haste.
H A variety of interests can stimulate conversation and maintain individuality.
I Excessive dependence on one's partner is unwise. He or she may be the first to die, or divorce may

occur; mutual responsibility enables *both* partners to cope, whatever happens.

Degrees of compatibility

Can any compatibility from A to I be improved? If so, how? Patient consideration and an honest appraisal from both parties could be put down on paper separately, then compared and discussed.

(Notes)

Doubtful compatibilityImprovement

SIGNS AND CONSEQUENCES OF LOW SELF-ESTEEM

Signs of low self-esteem are usually easy to spot in other people, but they are not so easy to detect in oneself because we are not always aware of our own attitudes, biases and preconceived notions. Here are some of the more common signs of low self-esteem we may perceive in friends and acquaintances:

A meek physical attitude when in the company of confident people.

*

Over-achieving, as in the case of someone who tried to make up for feelings of inadequacy in comparison with his brother by qualifying for four academic degrees: though at thirty-six he still lacked the confidence to risk an emotional commitment.

*

Maintaining a shabby appearance in support of feelings of inadequacy; or acting in the opposite way by overdressing in order to impress other people.

*

Avoiding responsibilities.

*

Lack of self-assertion and confidence in imitation, perhaps, of a parent.

*

A sense of inferiority, revealed by repeated self-criticism, due, perhaps to being convinced that one has not reached the standards set by parents, siblings or colleagues.

*

Bravado and ostentation, which are fairly obvious signs of low self-esteem.

A glance at the list so far may bring realisation of a personal trait that needs attention or, perhaps, the following sort of remedial action:

> Become conscious of your own qualities and aptitudes.
> Behave naturally: become aware of when you are trying to impress people.
> Attempt to understand why you have felt a need to prove you are *not* inferior; meditation on earlier experiences might help.

One of the worst effects of low self-esteem is that the outward signs, including those listed here, can be socially off-putting. They tend to create a distance between individuals who tip-toe fearfully through life, and those who stride confidently onward, despite inevitable setbacks and rejections.

PSYCHOLOGICAL INSIGHT INTO LOW SELF-ESTEEM.

At the risk of repetition, it is worth emphasising that psychological insight can be gained by dream association, an awareness of impulse behaviour, bringing reason to bear on 'excessive reactions'; noticing other people's unreasonable reactions, incidents of physical and mental tension, reading books or magazines on psychological matters and social relationships.

By taking meditational action on these antidotes to low self-esteem, you may come to realise why many low self-esteem situations arise and what can be done about them. This could make it easier to change negative attitudes.

Meditational self analysis can be assisted by the fact that subconsciously you know a lot more about yourself than you probably realise; it's worth repeating that you have within you, in mind and emotion, records of past events that can be, and in many cases should be linked up to your current attitudes and reactions. Dreams, for example, are not always significant, but their content can, on occasions, tell you what is worrying you, what you are hoping for, and whether some past happening needs to be exposed so that positive action can be taken or an attitude changed. An example of this latter point can be found in case histories quoted in another section of this book. Case history No7, in Part Three.

A simple and effective method of losing a giveaway sign of low self-esteem is to develop an outward appearance of confidence. These steps might be helpful:

- a) Open your mouth wider when speaking instead of mumbling.
- b) Look people in the eye while listening or speaking.
- c) Maintain an upright posture.
- d) Increase your knowledge: become well informed about something so that you are not lost for words during conversation.
- e) Try to find out the particular interests, desires or needs of the person you are with, and turn the conversation to them
- f) As already suggested, make use of dream material. Fairly common 'repeat' dreams are of inadequacy in various situations: missing a goal, standing alone when everyone around you has company, feeling lost and hopeless or arriving late for school with homework not yet done. See if you can remember a persistent theme in your personal dream catalogue, then meditate on it. By concentrating on the *feeling* experienced in such dreams and the nature of their content, you may by simple deduction get relevant realisations. When you begin to get happier, more positive dreams, it may be because things are starting to

look more promising; instead of rain and gloom, there is hope and sunshine.

g) In addition to acting on information from your subconscious, you can raise self esteem through auto-suggestions such as 'I am likeable, I am lovable, I am capable' as you picture things going right. I offer no apology for constantly repeating this particular slogan: its effectiveness in boosting confidence has been confirmed to me on a number of occasions.

Action required and intended

Notes

INSIGHTS AND FEELINGS

On a wall of the temple of Delphi in Ancient Greece, frequented by philosophers such as Plato and Socrates, there was a well known inscription: KNOW THYSELF. That frequently given advice is not only still valid but absolutely essential to the continuation of civilisation: a fact made alarmingly apparent when certain individuals, entrusted with almost unlimited power but with scant self-knowledge, caused millions of people to suffer the horrors of two World Wars.

If Stalin and Hitler had not been so ignorant about the drives and motives that governed their diabolical behaviour, they might have resolved emotional and psychological problems in a socially acceptable manner. The same is surely true of many unhappy people who languish behind bars in prisons all over the world.

Through books, magazines, newspapers, films and social experiences we can, of course, strive to specify the causes of unsocial behaviour in others and ourselves. But being able to bring new insights into effect can prove difficult if emotionally based concerns get in the way too often. A realisation of why one has suppressed anger does not get rid of it if that anger is not assuaged in any way by consideration or compassion.

Hitler's irate behaviour, for example, due possibly to feelings against his oppressive, bullying father, was so alarming during his early years in Vienna that it caused a relative to recommend psychological help. According to a newspaper article, he might have had a chance of being treated by Dr Sigmund Freud. We are left to wonder whether things could have turned out differently if the opportunity to gain self-knowledge had been taken.

Examples below show the power of emotion over reason.

Case number one: involved Miss W, who conveniently neglected to be sensitive to the feelings of others. The thing that prevented her from distinguishing right from wrong and the moral from the immoral was an emotional mist fostered by a needful desire. As a solicitor, trained to look at things rationally, Miss W should have been alarmed at the life she was leading but a need for love and affection marred her judgment and clouded her conscience.

Lonely and divorced, she had already parted two men from their wives and children and was at the point of causing a third marital break-up when she saw her current lover walking along with his wife and children. Stricken with guilt, she determined there and then to discover what lay behind her socially destructive conduct.

In her first session of psychotherapy, she was advised to find time to relax and meditate on the remark she had made that her mother and father had always been very close in their relationship.

By the following session, self-analysis had plainly revealed a core of jealousy and resentment over the lack of attention she had received as a child. 'I suppose I wanted to separate couples so that the husbands would give me the attention I needed,' she said. 'I can see now that they were figments of my childhood desire to have a father who cared and responded. I really do feel sorry about the unhappiness I've caused.'

After many years as a psychotherapist, I ceased to be surprised at the power of emotions to prevail over moral inclinations.

Case number two: Mr K was concerned that arguments with his wife might cause a serious break in their relationship. 'I love my wife,' he said, 'but I'm afraid of losing her. The trouble is I always have to be right, even when I know I'm not.' On being asked whether he'd ever known anyone who behaved in that way, he paused thoughtfully then, wide eyed, he exclaimed 'Yes, my father, and I think I know why! His own father would never let him win an argument.'

Anger was the emotional content in the verbal power struggles with his wife: the same anger and frustration his father had caused him to feel as a teenager.

Mr K was advised to consciously resist any *I'm right* impulse. With a little practice it got easier; they even joked about it after Mr K explained to his wife the reasons behind his need to be always right, and they saw a funny side to it when she revealed that her own excessive reaction had been because she too had been treated in the same way by her mother.

Case number three: involved Helen Sharman, Britain's first female astronaut, who was in a job that did not arouse much enthusiasm. She wanted to become intensively involved in something that would make her feel truly alive: a new experience. When the opportunity came she immediately applied, together with 13,000 like-minded applicants, for a chance to train for the Anglo Russian mission to enter outer space in March 1991. After rigorous tests and arduous training, she succeeded, much to her amazement, and finally boarded Soyuz TM-12.

During her breathtaking experience, as she viewed Planet Earth 250 miles away, Helen didn't only marvel at what she saw, she also thought of the admirable Russian people she had got to know while spending eighteen months in their company, and later commented:

'People are really all that matter wherever you are in the solar system. Nothing else is as important.'

She spoke of a feeling of spiritual affinity with people everywhere since her uplifting adventure in outer space, and later remarked:

'The worst thing that can happen in life is to feel nothing.'

How true! Without emotional expression we are only half alive.

Case number four: In the film *'Twelve Angry Men'*, one member of the jury voted 'guilty' in opposition to eleven others who had voted an accused young man 'innocent,' but he, the dissident member of the jury, had unknowingly transferred his anti-son feelings onto the similarly youthful defendant and was eventually forced into insight by a hysterical outburst in which he condemned teenagers who take for granted the sacrifices their parents make on their behalf. Reason ultimately triumphed over suppressed emotion, causing him, reluctantly, to cast a 'not guilty' verdict.

Case number five: revolves around Mr R, a dour, unresponsive man who wanted to pass on the family furniture business to his son but the young man was not in the least interested. Unfortunately, Mr R junior had been so starved of affection and was so in need of approval that when the time came for his father's retirement, the young man could not summon the moral courage to refuse his request to take over the business. He later realised that a need for acceptance and respect had caused him to waste fourteen of his best years doing work he thoroughly disliked.

Case number six: Despite her intelligence and sophistication, Miss S was puzzled and socially embarrassed by an unreasonable fear of being left alone. But, empowered by desperation, she finally obtained assistance .After several sessions of psychotherapy, an important memory surfaced while she was undergoing hypnotic regression:-

'I'm in a pram at the far end of a garden' she said, 'Mother has left me alone. I'm afraid. I don't know whether I'll ever see her again.'

Her years of insecurity appeared to date from this incident because afterwards, she gradually became aware that being alone was no longer a matter for concern.

In order to consolidate her newfound sense of security. she was encouraged to mentally repeat several times prior to sleep: *'Solitude can be relaxing, peaceful and creative'* while she imagined enjoyable periods of peace and contentment. After a few days she declared herself to be satisfied that the problem was solved.

Dreams enable us to unload anger, guilt and fear, as well as wishes, frustrations and intentions.

Case number seven: Mr J had a repeat dream of firing a gun at another person. When asked to picture the aggressor's name being written on a blackboard, he was amazed to discover that the gunman was himself and the victim was his brother. This dream enabled Mr J to realise what lay behind the puzzling hostility he felt towards his good-natured brother. Psychotherapy uncovered how much he had resented his rival sibling for appearing to steal most of their parents' affection and esteem. Therapy also revealed why he had always been an attention-seeker with a subconscious wish to be noticed and appreciated as much as his brother.

In consequence of this realisation, he was able to accept that previous resentment against his brother was emotional rather than rational. Many people might find it difficult to believe that a straightforward case of sibling rivalry was not apparent to Mr J at a much earlier stage in life; perhaps conscience has caused him to repress recognition of his jealousy.

IN FEAR OF LOVE

Those who have never been loved, not even in childhood, tend to be over-cautious about emotional commitment and are liable to believe themselves to be unacceptable or unlovable. People with this attitude may settle for an amicable partnership based on mutual values, shared interests, companionship and loyalty, as so many people do.

But the following example is of someone who was not prepared to compromise. Mr J was determined to do something about his emotional frigidity even if it meant going back to painful memories.

'Didn't your parents show any affection at all?' I asked.

'No' was his curt reply, 'and I never saw any sign of warmth or concern between them.'

It was not surprising that he lacked confidence and self-esteem: words of encouragement were, it seems, as rare as a butterfly on an iceberg in his home environment.

'As I was leaving home' he said, 'I realised more clearly than ever how emotionally uptight my mother was as she tried to hold back a tear. It was sad and infuriating to know that she hadn't the guts over all those years to let me know she cared, but hark at me talking. I've turned out to be just as bad. Like her, I'm dead scared of showing my feelings in case I get hurt.'

Mr T looked older than his thirty-eight years: stooped shoulders, almost inaudible speech and downcast eyes made it easy to see why he found it difficult to make friends.

He was advised to meditate periodically for several weeks on various defences he had been using in order to avoid emotional involvement: staying indoors too much and too often, for instance, turning down social opportunities or spending an inordinate amount of time on trivial or unimportant matters. Mr T endeavoured to do this, having realised that action was long overdue, and was informed that he had reason for optimism because by generating hope, he was moving away from the Red Zone of confusion and despair.

BARRIERS TO LIKEABILITY AND LOVABILITY

The following barriers to L and Lo could be helpful in recognising whatever may be standing in the way of things you want or need to achieve, including social acceptance:
1. Avoiding opportunities to attend social activities by convincing yourself you would not know what to say.
2. Risking financial viability by extravagant misuse of money or using drugs, alcohol or some other type of harmful diversion as an excuse, perhaps, to avoid life's challenges.
3. Being a taker and not a giver is a way of showing that you are too self-centred, and a poor choice of partner.
4. Being a snob, a bully or a boaster may categorise you as an unpleasant person with a serious inferiority or superiority complex.
5. A social partnership is not likely to succeed if one person is unreliable, lazy or too dependent.
6. Lack of kindness, generosity or consideration may imply an inability to get beyond *self*, due to emotional immaturity.

7. A morose, introverted and negative personality is most likely to prove a strong deterrent to anyone on the lookout for cheerful, humorous companionship.
8. Failing to see another person's point of view or respect their individuality.
9. Lack of moral fibre
10. Low moral standard: not to be trusted

Perhaps you should ask yourself:
1. Am I self righteous and bigoted because, due to lack of confidence I cannot admit to being wrong or is it because my mother/father seldom allowed me to be right?
2. Am I intolerant because my mind is closed to opinions that might make me question long-held beliefs, attitudes and values?
3. Am I a boring workaholic because my work helps to shut out the emotional vacuum in my life or is it that I value myself only as an achiever?
4. Why am I unable to relax? Is my lifestyle out of balance in terms of work fulfilment, health, recreation, values, social life or closeness to nature?
5. Or do I need individual psychotherapy?
6. Why do I get unreasonably jealous? Is it because I have such a low opinion of myself that I cannot believe anyone could possibly be in love with me; and that therefore my partner must be having an affair with someone else?
7. Why do I lack courage and determination? Perhaps excessive criticism and lack of praise in childhood destroyed my self-belief; maybe I'm afraid of the

responsibilities that marriage or promotion would bring.
8. I'm inclined to be rather remote. Perhaps I keep people at a distance because I'm afraid of criticism, of not being acceptable or being let down.
9. Am I prudish due to a narrow-minded upbringing, with a strong religious bias toward sexual taboos, guilt and unworthiness?
10. Am I unable to socialise with the opposite sex because I went to a single-sex school, because my parents were unsociable or because I'm still living at home and haven't had the courage to assert my independence?
11. Do I transfer anti-parent feelings onto members of the opposite gender?
12. Do I associate marriage and social commitment with loss of independence?

Most people could find faults and fallibilities within themselves without a great deal of searching. It may be possible, through meditation, to unearth a personal barrier to likeability additional to those quoted here. Several case histories relative to the above questions are included throughout these pages, also auto-suggestions that may enable you to change negative feelings into positive, hopeful attitudes through brief repetitions of the slogan: *I am likeable, I am lovable, I am capable.* These and other encouraging phrases can raise self-esteem to some extent, regardless of whether you believe them; though ideally, you should do everything you can to justify their intended effect.

It is highly unlikely that many people would need to take

action on all the barriers to likeability but in any case the required action is not always difficult. For instance, in number three, 'being a taker and not a giver', you can determine to overcome the problem simply by becoming sincerely more generous .If, on the other hand, you think number three does not apply, you can pose yourself these questions:-

a) Do I use people for what I can get out of them?
b) Do I ever consider another person's rights and needs as much as I do my own?
c) When did I last perform an act of kindness or generosity without thought of reward?
d) Do I sometimes give praise or encouragement or am I too critical and judgemental?

Looking at a day or a week in retrospect, whether at home or at work, may make it easier to find appropriate answers. If you have to admit to lack of affection, consideration, or general regard for others, yet do not understand why, you may be in need of a dramatic psychological or philosophical adjustment. Barrier number six, *getting beyond self* (a litmus paper test for degrees of likeability) might be a barrier worthy of your best efforts to overcome social problems.

Barriers I Intend to Overcome

Your personal barrier may not have been listed overleaf but most emotional and psychological problems are connected to fears and anxieties. If you meditate patiently, joining up present troubles with past related happenings, you could hit upon a clue to your outstanding barrier.

Barrier	Realisation	Action taken

TRANSCENDENTAL ABSOLUTION FROM ANTI-SOCIAL FEELINGS

Psychotherapy or counselling can be effective procedures for coming to terms with troubles such as irrational anger, hate, envy or revengeful feelings, but the following method of exorcising emotional leeches such as those just mentioned might be helpful to people who have failed to respond to conventional therapies.

To forgive a person because of some sort of pious duty could be insincere or hypocritical; but to free yourself of anger, hate or revengeful feelings that stand in the way of likeability, lovability and peace of mind by sincerely using a method that transcends normal or physical experience is another matter and may prove to be well worth the time involved. The procedure is as follows:

1. Sit near to pebbles that are being clawed back into the sea.
2. Hold a fistful of them firmly in one hand.
3. With imagination and intense concentration, transfer the feelings you sincerely want to be rid of into those tightly held pebbles. Having wilfully purged yourself of unwanted feelings, hurl the

       stones containing those feelings into the sea.
4. Listen to the waves, with closed eyes, as they drag the vice-embodied pebbles further and further away, setting you free.
5. This method may help people afflicted with an emotional malaise for which they have found no answer, be it religious, psychological or medical.

Because we function mentally and morally (as well as emotionally), transcendental absolution should be backed up by attitudes and actions that are the opposite of hate, greed, jealousy, revengeful feelings or any other vices that have been embodied in sea pebbles.

OVERCOMING NEGATIVE STRESS

Titanic courage

Whatever your most stressful task or responsibility may be, compare it with one faced by musicians on board the sloping deck of the sinking Titanic as they continued to play music in an effort to calm panicking passengers. Equally fearful of their own imminent death in an icy sea, they used concentration, willpower and courage, but they dared not use *imagination;* if they had, they would probably have joined the desperate passengers in search of a lifeboat.

The incredible moral courage of those selfless musicians on the doomed Titanic passenger liner is surely comparable with the courageous self-sacrificing act of the noble Burghers of Calais, commemorated so splendidly by Rodin the sculptor (1984-1917), a copy of which can be seen at Embankment Gardens at Westminster, London. One day, perhaps, the modest musicians' noble act may also be commemorated in stone or paint.

Imagination can be a useful and valid tool in circumstances that involve anxiety and stress, when coolness and courage

are needed at a business meeting for example, or when an important presentation has to be made to impress a group of people. In demanding situations like these it can be helpful to repeat in thought or word the following auto-suggestion while relaxing and visualising the scene:
I'll do well. I'm looking forward to it.

And borrow a tip from actors about to go on stage: regulate your breathing by taking a couple of deep breaths immediately beforehand and think:
I'm relaxed and confident

Stress and Imagination

Stress can be defined as a state of mental, emotional or physical strain; if it is heightened by pictorial thoughts of a negative nature, the cumulative effect on vital organs can be so strong as to produce the sort of result that occurred when Israelis were bombarded with Scud missiles. It was suspected at the time that the missiles might contain a deadly gas. This naturally caused great anxiety among people in areas within their range.

It was later reported that the average heart mortality rate rose by an astonishing 58 per cent, though the actual death toll caused by the missiles was only a tiny fraction of that percentage. The main killer, it seems, was fear, magnified by *imagination*. When the victims' blood pressure got to a certain level, it probably brought on heart attacks or strokes in vulnerable people.

To a lesser extent, anger and anxiety can, as is well known, raise blood pressure to an unacceptable level if a person is overweight, smokes, gets insufficient exercise or does not have regular medical check-ups.

Capability is also liable to be affected if people fail to take steps to avoid negative stress: for example, leaving without enough time for the daily journey to work by bus, train or car.

Thoughts can control emotions, lower blood pressure and moderate the heart beat rate, so instead of fuming at traffic lights or traffic jams, just think:

I'm calm and relaxed

Patience is not only a virtue, it is also a tranquillizer that can save lives.

PEACE OF MIND IN 100 SECONDS
Stress and relaxation

If you are overwrought and constantly buzzing with mental activity, peace of mind may not come easily.

A good technique for stilling the mind is to sit or lie in a quiet place as you mentally count to 100, blocking every thought that threatens to intervene by picturing each consecutive number. Some people may require patient practice before achieving 100 thoughtless seconds; others might attain their target of mental vacuity more quickly.

Before you start counting, think:
'When I get to my personal target of seconds, I shall be wonderfully relaxed and peaceful'.

While in that mentally receptive state, allow your mind to *receive* any random memory or dream, however, far back; it might enable you to link up with a current stress situation like the one featured in case history No 7, on page 117 and the Stress and Capability section page 132 overleaf.

One hundred thoughtless seconds, with mental and visual

concentration on each digit, can create a suitable state for the application of auto-suggestions.

STRESS AND CAPABILITY

As already mentioned, past and present are often linked by the same emotion.

Mr H, a much-journeyed businessman, suddenly developed an irrational fear of air travel. Greatly puzzled and very concerned, he urgently required help, anxious that the phobia might cost him his job. On being asked, while in a state of hypnosis, to trace his fearful feelings back as far as possible, he hit upon a memory that had been hidden for many years. 'I'm nine,' he said. 'I'm ever so scared. I'm on a Big Dipper at a seaside fair. It's going up and down very fast. I'm afraid of being flung into the sea'.

He was told: 'You're in the same Big Dipper but this time your trip will be lots of fun, you'll feel safe and confident.'

His expression at the end of the imaginary trip showed that he was no longer afraid of being tossed into the sea.

But Mr H still failed to understand why a past experience had made such an impact for no apparent reason. The reason was not apparent because the repressed memory of not being in control was emotionally linked with being miles away when his wife was due to have her baby. In such a situation he would have been out of control, just as in the Big Dipper experience all those years ago; 'control' and 'flying' had become closely linked in his mind and with associated feelings.

Fortunately, his boss, also a family man, was very understanding and grounded him till his wife had given birth.

A telephone call several weeks after he became a father made it clear to me that he had lost the associated fear of not being in control.

Although anxiety and stress do not always impair capability, they can impede thought and action - during a driving test, for instance, when the learner may freeze at the wheel and lose control. But by imagining yourself relaxed, confident and fully concentrated on the task, you can pre-empt a dreaded situation by telling yourself:

I am calm and confident

Assertions of confidence and reassurance should, of course, be reinforced by ability and effort. Auto-suggestion cannot be a substitute for capability, but it may enable you to be at your best in various situations.

If you are using auto-suggestion for a driving test you should, for public safety, first get an assurance from your instructor that you have gained the necessary skills and know the driving code. And if you are prone to road rage or panic, you may need to get psychological help before taking a driving test.

BOREDOM AND STRESS

Some people think it is stressful to be bored but that depends how boredom affects you. Far from always being a dull and uninteresting condition, boredom can sometimes produce a fertile state for inventive ideas, themes for authors and inspirational tunes for composers of music If we are bored, the mind is not racing around like a dog chasing its tail.

Milton's *Paradise Lost*, Oscar Wilde's *Ballad of Reading Gaol*, Hitler's *Mein Kampf* and numerous other writings (whether wise or unwise) were written in the most boring of all environments: four walls and the bars of a prison cell, in an unhurried situation wherein a person can reach out into the realms of fantasy and realisation beyond the boundaries of doubt and discouragement; a place where periodic tedium can be extremely relaxing for a tired brain.

Even boredom of a negative sort can jerk a person into activity if that individual is stirred by desperation over circumstances that must be changed.

One advantage from an analytical point of view is that while in a languid state when silence prevails, contemplation can provide answers to psychological or emotional problems, rather like a squirrel uncovering a long-buried acorn.

HARMFUL PRENATAL INFLUENCES

Most parents do everything in their power to ensure the prenatal health and welfare of their future offspring, but some of them choose to ignore warnings of mental and physical defects that can be caused by smoking, alcohol and drugs.

Professor Peter Hopper of Queen's University, Belfast has expressed alarm at the growing body of evidence linking brain damage to alcohol. He maintains that if a pregnant woman drinks even small amounts of alcohol it, may cause her baby to suffer brain damage.

*

As is fairly well known, if a mother smokes, her unborn child may suffer from respiratory problems for an indefinite period of time.

*

The potential consequences of pregnant women taking illicit drugs can be truly tragic; traces of cannabis and other drugs have been detected in the bloodstream of infants. Having a baby who enters the world as an addict, is possibly brain-damaged through the effects of alcohol, or who is predestined to have asthma or some other respiratory disease, in spite of health warnings, is disgraceful self-centeredness, bordering on criminal negligence or at the very least, emotional immaturity.

*

The consequences of causing preventable ill health can of course be far-reaching and long-lasting in terms of a child's chances of happiness and fulfilment. Unfortunately, the time has not yet arrived for obligatory prenatal education to be accepted as common practice in schools.

SOCIAL INFLUENCES ON CHILDREN
Peer Pressure

It could be assumed that only ignorant or uncaring mothers would cause harmful things to happen to their children and that intelligent, educated, socially privileged young people should not fall victim to the sort of peer pressure that caused a prosperous woman's daughter to be forcibly detained under the Mental Health act at a Manchester hospital. But her daughter's need for self-esteem and companionship proved to be stronger than common sense or parental example. The distraught mother gave this warning to parents:

'I thought that by not making a big deal of Catherine's smoking of dope and by not turning it into a forbidden fruit I was doing the right thing. Now I regret not putting my foot down because the guilt and recrimination I feel is overwhelming.'

Catherine's cannabis-induced psychosis caused her to be confused and aggressive. She was, therefore, less likeable, probably less lovable and most probably less capable.

A major problem for parents is that drug addiction is not always easy to detect initially; unwary users may be seduced by cannabis, a mind-bending substance that masquerades as a harmless, relaxing comforter. But it should carry a warning: *If you use now, you'll pay later.*

OBESITY
A Matter of Life or Death

Obesity in the USA is in macabre competition with smoking for the dishonour of being the nation's number one killer; and according to statistics, Britain is likely to follow suit. Becoming fat is usually such a gradual process that a parent who fails to check a child's weight increase risks potential damage to that child's LLoC, or much worse.

In 2002 there was only a brief press reference to the suicide of an overweight thirteen-year-old girl. The reference was brief because the situation is not uncommon, therefore not particularly newsworthy. The girl took her own life because school bullies called her insulting names and led her to believe that nobody liked her. The fact that an identical tragedy had occurred in the same year gives some indication of the sort of humiliation, isolation and despair that some overweight children have to endure. Both girls were probably loved; but love was not enough. If the girls' parents had heeded pubic warnings about sensible eating, the girls might not have died due to parental ignorance, neglect, or the absence of health checks at home and at school.

Maintain Your Capability by Preventing Obesity

Be mindful of the fact that obesity can creep up on you as stealthily as a mountain mist. If you are in denial of an overweight condition you might subconsciously ignore the following signs: (obvious though they may be.)

An unflattering appearance

Clothes that have become too tight

Discomfort in the abdomen

Shortness of breath

Aching legs and swollen ankles

Eating more than you need

A reluctance to exercise

You might also fail to take the precaution of having regular cholesterol and blood pressure checks.

As you get older and do less exercise, food requirement diminishes; so the amount of calories you consume should (according to medical opinion) not exceed the amount of calories used in exercise and daily routine if you wish to achieve and maintain a healthy weight.

If you are anxious or depressed, lonely or bored be wary of trying to console yourself with unnecessary snacks which can pile on surplus calories and significantly expand your waistline beyond and in defiance of your doctor's recommendation. Try, instead to busy yourself in something useful or interesting. This could make mindless munching less likely. It can be helpful to keep a Things To Do list within easy reach.

Doctors are in general of the opinion that overweight people should eat less and exercise more often. 'Easier said than done' you might think. But try self analysis. When you stuff yourself with fatty foods, pause; question what was going on in your mind and feelings when you got the self-destructive urge. Was it related to anger, loneliness, boredom or an affront to your self-esteem? If not, what *was* going through your mind? If your answer is 'nothing', relax and search your memory once again because it is very difficult to think of nothing. Identifying a current feeling may lead more easily to a link with mindless munching.

Quite often overeating or excess drinking is triggered off by undue criticism, unkind remarks or emotionally based situations that affect a person's sense of security in any way. School children in particular are known to suffer by insults if they are noticeably over-weight; they may not take to drinking or drugs during childhood but I have known numerous adults who have traced lack of confidence and self-assertion to hurtful words said long ago.

Well adjusted people are more likely to be in harmony with their instinctive urges; if you are unable to specify which of your basic instincts is not being fulfilled the Herd (social instinct) will probably come to mind. When you have taken steps to put things right (either within yourself and your attitude to life), or your local community, you may be more inclined to eat less and do regular physical exercises with increased vigour and determination.

Willpower undoubtedly can be strengthened by auto-suggestions such as

I have no need or desire for big meals or fattening foods. Smaller meals give me a full-up satisfying feeling

By also using smaller plates you can steer yourself away from obesity and with the addition of regular exercise you may avoid the dreaded prospect of becoming chair bound and dependent in old age. It would be helpful to get approval from your doctor for measures you take to reduce weight, mentioning any pills or supplements you are taking.

Why don't more people use their willpower?

- Perhaps they use worries about obesity as a distraction from problems they would rather not think about.
- Fear of sex or emotional commitment may cause them to wilfully appear unattractive and wary, or be unwilling to change.
- From earliest childhood food is associated with comfort, love and survival. Emotional insecurity causes some people to seek comfort by filling an emotional void with sweet things such as cakes and chocolate 'if nobody loves me I'll love myself'.
- Some people delude themselves into thinking that diabetes affects only *other* people. Obesity can of course be due to physical malfunction.
- If obesity is emotionally embedded, people

subconsciously might not wish to exercise willpower and could be in need of psychotherapy.

Some people, may not realise the potential power of 'self help' through willpower, but if you put the following slogan on your wall so that you are constantly reminded of it, your mind may accept, however reluctantly, that:

weight can usually be reduced by eating less and by daily exercise.

You can programme your mind to solve some of the things that puzzle you. As you drop off to sleep ask yourself 'Why have I been eating more than I need?' Or some such relevant question. You might then find yourself dreaming a dream that provides a link to whatever emotional attachment there may have been to your attitude toward food. The answer may be factual or symbolic.

By thinking, as you drop off to sleep, 'I'll remember my dreams', you tap into the search engine within. You can then write down whatever you've remembered when you awake: using that dream material as a source for meditation when the time is convenient.

INFLUENCING YOUR LIFESPAN

An internationally respected Nurses' Health Study included the monitoring of 44,702 women over a period of eight years. One conclusion from this important study by the Harvard Medical School was that fat around the abdomen is linked to heart problems.

It appears that waist measurement should be no more than half your height. Beyond that limit, health risks begin to increase. Anyone who is unsure about weight and waist statistics should get a personal assessment from their doctor.

Health reports suggest that self-control, regular exercise, caution over fatty comfort foods and an adequate daily portion of fruit and vegetables should reduce waistline measurements, thereby minimising risks of heart disease and diabetes.

It is not advisable to use smoking as a means of reducing appetite because even 20 cigarettes per day is deemed to be the equivalent in health terms of carrying an extra stone in weight.

THE RETURN OF DIEGO MARADONA

Will and motivation

Diego Maradona, the world-renowned footballer, is no longer a nineteen-stone has-been with no self-discipline. Through commendable strength of will, he had an operation which enabled him to lose eight stone, and through self-discipline he regained physical fitness, becoming nimble and energetic enough to enter a dance competition – leading with his famous left foot in a romantic Argentine dance, the Tango. We can only hope that, despite the constant pressure of coping with fame, he will be able to maintain his greatly improved condition.

How did Diego, after so many years, finally acquire the strength of mind to reject illicit drugs, exercise excessively, and restrict his intake of food?

'It's not so much thanks to any clinic or any doctor. It's for the love of my daughters. I've been saved by love,' he said.

Claudia Villafane, his wife, also played an important part. The love of his family eventually made him see how self-centred he had been: and what his self-inflicted death would have meant to them .It was the release from *self* that gave him the necessary courage and determination to reject drugs and eat moderately, and his *will* was strengthened when he found the right motivation.

Overweight or addicted people may draw strength and hope from Maradona's example. They might also make good use of the slogan on the next page whenever they need courage and determination to face up to a difficult situation

You may currently be short of money and success, but will, motivation, positive thoughts and the use of imagination can be reinforced by this autosuggestion which could easily be rephrased to deal with other issues such as reaching weight reduction targets or qualifying for a career.

I CAN AND I WILL

Past generations have realised that certain slogans can, especially when seen or spoken repeatedly, strongly influence the way we think and the way we feel. Advertisers make use of this technique, so why shouldn't you?

INFLUENCING YOUR CHILD'S LIFESPAN

Passive smoking: In 2005 a national newspaper headline read:-
    THE BOY WITH THE LUNGS OF A PENSIONER

A five-year-old child's respiratory system was badly damaged by cigarette fumes. His cigarette-addicted mother was full of sorrow and regret for her son's lamentable condition and made a belated attempt to overcome her ingrained habit.

She was herself a victim of parental example, as were her two sisters and a brother who became heavy smokers. It is no exaggeration to say that of all the tobacco-addicted people I interviewed, over 70 per cent had parents who smoked.

Because of his mother's addiction, the five-year-old boy could have been a passive smoker while still in the womb. A spokesman for ASH, an Action on Smoking organisation, said that:
'just because you smoke in a different room of the house it doesn't mean harm isn't being done. Closing the door won't work.'

It is worth mentioning, as a footnote, that the lungs of dogs and cats are, unsurprisingly, also harmfully affected by tobacco smoke.

A summary of beneficial Survival Targets: in relation to commonly ignored medical advice:

- **If necessary, reduce your waist to a medically recommended size.**
- **Increase daily exercise by how much?**
- **Eat healthier meals: with effect from what date?**
- **Get regular check-ups on blood pressure, weight and cholesterol levels.**
- **Make your home a no-smoking zone.**
- **Ensure, as far as possible, that the family stays at a healthy weight and gets plenty of exercise.**
- **Ensure that you get enough sleep and recreation.**

THE POWERS OF A BABY

When Elizabeth Barrett Browning wrote:

'How do I love thee?'
'Let me count the ways',

she did not have babies in mind, but those famous lines do sum up the adoring gaze and tender feelings of millions of mothers as they hold in their arms the most beautiful baby in the world while revelling in the joys of motherhood. However, behind a baby's trusting, wide-eyed innocence there lurks a power that is very real indeed.

Prenatal considerations
1. Babies have the power to cause jealousy and insecurity in any member of the family, not always on a conscious level.
2. But they can also enable any member of the family to become more mature, less self-centred.
3. A baby generally adds more meaning and purpose to its parents' lives.
4. It can cause its mother to give up an interesting, well-paid job and become reconciled to living on a lower income.

5. Father may bristle with pride and become more determined to be financially secure. Because of deep feelings and new responsibilities, he may spend less time drinking alcohol. Wishing to be a good example, he might even stop smoking in order to avoid causing his child respiratory problems.
6. Physically or mentally imperfect babies may cause their parents to react with bitterness and resentment, but some parents are spiritually strengthened by their efforts to cope emotionally and financially.
7. Babies demonstrate how childish we may appear when we show jealousy, rage and selfishness.
8. Babies make most parents feel needed, loved and valued. Wealth and success may have eluded many new mothers and fathers but babies generally compensate by bringing the fun and laughter that money cannot buy.
9. People who are convinced of the finality of death may find consolation in having their genes carried on into future generations; a phenomenon associated in some eastern cultures with traditional adherence to a belief in reincarnation.
10. Grandparents are generally rejuvenated by the arrival of a grandchild and are usually willing to be of assistance, whether through giving unwanted advice or by lending a helping hand.
11. A baby's biggest impact is usually of course on its mother. Conversely, it is generally the mother who makes the biggest emotional impact on the baby by her care, her moral standards and whether or not she, together with her partner, is emotionally able

to convince her child of its likeability, lovability and capability. Although a father's influence is often limited by the time and energy spent at work, he does appear to represent men in general; therefore, his capacity for love and affection is likely to affect his child's emotional wellbeing for years to come, especially where daughters are concerned.

12. Innovative engineers, architects, poets, composers of music, artists, writers and inventors experience the exhilaration of creativity but how does their elation compare with the feelings of a woman when she creates a baby? She is enriched emotionally, mentally and spiritually; spiritually in the sense that her collusion with nature has fulfilled a function for which she is admirably equipped and mentally and emotionally endowed; often with increased tolerance, humour and selfless devotion.

13. Her baby has conferred upon her the honour and privilege of motherhood and presents an opportunity for both parents to express unconditional love.

14. Invariably a baby bestows happiness and pride on its parents and awakens in them a newfound determination to overcome whatever problems may arise. I once said to a builder perched up on a ladder: 'But how on earth do you cope with five children?'

    'If you have to, you do' he replied.

15. A baby can also awaken an emotional intensity that might not otherwise have been experienced, infusing its parents with feelings they never knew they had.

16. Its mother may have regarded herself as a woman of no importance, but motherhood has changed all that: she is now a goddess, needed, liked and loved.
17. As a parent, you will probably need to adjust your aims and the priority of your values. Your baby may thereby alter the course of your life.
18. You may need to move to larger accommodation near a good school.
19. Your in-laws now have a personal interest: your baby shares their genes.
20. Your baby's behaviour should cause you to become better informed in childcare, and more psychologically aware of your own capacity for patience, endurance and selflessness.
21. A wise man once said: 'Unless you become as little children you shall not enter the kingdom of Heaven'. The so-called Kingdom of Heaven may be revealed to parents by very small children through their disarming honesty in the things they say; their lack of false pride; their unqualified acceptance of other children; and their willingness to love.
22. When you see a smile on the face of a woman pushing a pram, it is probably due to the fact that she is fulfilled through the expression of *instincts* such as:
23. **Pride:** over her new status as a mother. With her partner, she is usually willing to take on vitally important family responsibilities.
24 **Tenderness:** This can change a tiger into a pussycat and a coward into a hero.
25. **Assertion:** Many young women are denied

opportunities for self-assertion at work; but there can be few better ways of expressing oneself than by creating a human being.

26. **Social:** A social bonus is that mothers generally like to talk to each other about their offspring, leading to an exchange of information and, often, new friendships.

27. **Sex:** A sexually and emotionally fulfilled mother has experienced a physical and mental phase of development that cannot naturally be attained in any other way; she and her partner, as parents, are additionally endowed with the privilege of helping to shape the character and health of another human being.

MARRIAGE OR COHABITATION

Rejection and abuse in childhood has made many people wary of marriage and emotional commitment, causing them to opt for cohabitation. Unfortunately, cohabitation has many drawbacks. Patricia Morgan, senior research fellow of the Institute for the Study of Civil Society, points out that in Britain, (2000+):

'Four out of ten single-parent families now spring from "live together" relationships which have no legal, moral or emotional commitment', and that 'both partners are likely to finish up living alone'. In her book *Marriage Lite: the Rise of Cohabitation*, she states:

'6.4 % of cohabiting females say they are the victims of domestic violence, compared with
2.7% of married women'.

Her research showed that children with married parents do better at school academically and sociably, and that three-quarters of children with cohabiting parents committed criminal offences compared with only a quarter from married parents. This appalling ratio appears to confirm a fairly well-known fact: that a high percentage of illiterate prison inmates come from break-ups in cohabiting relationships.

This is not surprising when one considers how difficult it can be for a child to understand and cope while lacking the emotional support of a cohabiting parent.

The absence of a loving parent is likely to be regarded as rejection, no matter what explanations or excuses may be offered. One young lady remarked bitterly:

'I have never forgiven him [her father] for deserting me; I'm not prepared to trust any man again.'

The loss of self-esteem that the absence of a parent can bring is not easy to overcome unless the remaining parent is encouraging, has psychological insight and a sufficiently loving nature to bring to a child a real sense of worth.

The author Patricia Morgan may appear to have a biased attitude towards cohabiting, but her claims are based on lengthy research and corroborative statistics. No matter what reservations people my have over those stated statistics, cohabitation is surely a choice that should not be taken too lightly, bearing in mind the possible impact on a child's likeability, lovability and general approach to life.

So what can be done? I have tentatively suggested issues of a preventative nature in the section 'Choosing a Suitable Partner', but in the long run the most we can do is to try to be emotionally aware and as psychologically enlightened as possible in the hope that relationships, based on firmer foundations, will successfully survive.

PART FOUR

Frank Sinatra's Farewell Message

Frank Sinatra's farewell message came fortuitously in the form of a song that expressed the desire of many of his generation in the USA and Europe to make the most of life after the devastating and limiting effects of WW2 during which, in Europe, millions of people were deprived of freedom and the right to openly declare what they truly felt and believed.

The song *My Way* is tantamount to a declaration of independence. With the exception of Edith Piaf, it is difficult to name anyone who could have equalled Sinatra's ardent rendering of it. The words could not have been expressed with such conviction by a younger singer who had not lived through the war years. Its message is, in effect:-

Don't allow yourself to become an impressionable piece of clay: easily manipulated. Through **self-determination** *you can more effectively live life to the full. If you do not hold on to free will and independence you may forfeit the right to express the way you truly feel and what you really believe; leaving yourself vulnerable to bureaucrats and dictators who are prepared to do your thinking for you.*

Some people presumed that because the song was so suited to Sinatra's character and personality it must have been written specially for him. Not so. Paul Anker admired the style and melody of the French song by Revaux and Gilles Thibault and decided to fit his own lyrics to the melody. He then looked for a suitable singer.

Frank, the Stradivarius of Pop singers, never wore a suit

This picture was taken in 1997 when, in a more philosophical mood, Sinatra stirred minds and hearts of people all over the world with his greatest hit:
MY WAY

Sinatra's voice, style and personality made him, periodically, the most popular and recognisable person in the English speaking world. For over 50 years his incomparable renderings of romantic songs soothed many a troubled brow and probably brought many a flicker to many a dying flame.

that fitted him as well as the style and pace of the music and the memorable lyrics provided by Paul Anker. The words embody Sinatra's gutsy, courageous spirit and his determination to live life to the full – come what may; if this book could have half the regenerating effect of *My Way* on people's self-determination, the author would feel amply rewarded for three years of effort.

It is not difficult to understand why Sinatra's greatest hit still echoes across frontiers. It applies to people everywhere: young and old, who have been held back frustrated and disheartened by lack of confidence and the challenges and injustices of life, who still hope for what might be and what could be.

In a 1935 film of The Mutiny on the Bounty a dying member of the ship's crew was being comforted. With his last breath he muttered: 'Nothing lost, Mr Christian'. The last words of Frank Sinatra 'I'm losing it.' (in more fortunate times) showed his marked reluctance to let go of life. Judging by the way he sang *My Way* he wanted everyone else to live as fully as he had done: with self-determination and a mind of their own. CIA came naturally to him. Like the rest of us he was not perfect, but he walked the Yellow Brick Road with a smile on his face, despite the setbacks and heartaches that life had to offer.

HAVE YOU SURRENDERED YOUR MIND?

Self-determination, ***the process by which people can control their lives***, is a right too precious to be negligently surrendered. Yet millions of people surrender their minds by passively and uncritically following the cultural beliefs and traditions of their parents or a diktat *imposed* by a religious or political body in power. In addition to this, the effects of emotional manipulation by politicians, corporations, the media, convention and peer pressure can pose a threat to free-thinking and free will; but so can ignorance, apathy, lack of psychological insight, bad parenting and lack of moral courage.

Peer Power: an enticement to conform

Controlling your own life is easier said than done. Peer pressure in some parts of the world is strongly linked with a country's cultural expectations and pressure to comply. Afghanistani women, for example, face extremely harsh penalties if they dare to challenge obligatory customs. But a more subtle type of pressure to conform happens in the West, as the following example shows:

A very distressed lady was afraid to fall asleep at night; yet according to her doctor there was no apparent reason for her sleeplessness. 'What do you fear most?' I enquired, having failed to find any clue to her distressing condition. 'I'm afraid that if I die in my sleep I'll go to Hell,' she replied. 'I've not been a good Catholic; I don't go to church any more.'

The relief on her face was obvious when I showed her the following excerpt from a speech made by the current Pope, which appeared in the national press on July 29, 1999:

'There's no such place as hell,' said Pope John Paul. *'Hell is not a physical place. And Heaven is not up in the clouds.'*

'If I were to ditch the beliefs handed down to me,' she said, 'it would be difficult because most of my friends and relatives still stick to the religion they've always followed.

Fear of not conforming to the lifestyle of friends and parents certainly played a part in her sustained semblance of being a 'good' Catholic. But that was not the whole story; she lacked the courage to face and investigate religious fears that were instilled during childhood. It was yet another example of emotion overcoming reason.

Peer pressure can obviously be harmful enough to deserve serious attention if, as an enticement to conform, it becomes an obstacle to the control of your own life. In her important book *The Nurture Assumption*, Judy Harris questions the view that nurture has the greatest effect in the long term on behavioural attitudes. She claims, after years of research, that peer pressure is equally if not more significant than parental influence.

Children do not of course share the same priorities and interests as adults; they tend to turn to their own age group for approval, understanding and a sense of belonging. My own daughter was very upset by the death of the family's beloved cat but instead of turning to parents who shared her feelings, she sought solace from a nine-year-old schoolmate.

'It's very difficult to avoid drugs in my social setting; everyone else is taking them,' said a young student from a well-known, privileged family. Parental and educational advice had failed to save him from a potentially fatal addiction. A need to fit in and be accepted caused him to go against wise counsel and his own common sense.

Pressure to conform: through manipulation of basic instincts

A monumental example of pressure to conform and imitate occurred during the Second World War. In Nazi Germany, Hitler capitalised on people's herd ('go with the pack') instinct as a means of persuasion. Even intellectually superior citizens succumbed emotionally to his tedious, repetitious rhetoric, which eventually convinced the German people that they should follow their leader. Through control of the media he was able to superimpose on them his own warped standards and feelings by triggering instinctual reactions of pride, fear and hatred with statements such as:

'I represent you, the German people; you represent me. The national interest is best served, therefore, when you follow me, your leader.'

Individuality was discouraged by incitement to national pride and vanity. The German people, he claimed, are a master race. Moral objections were seemingly overcome by the implication that God supported their cause. With an assumed agenda that absolutely anything was justified in order to save the Fatherland, newspapers were censored and radio broadcasts continually pressed home the need for unity against those who opposed Nazi ideologies. Uncritical compliance was demanded. Swastikas and 'Heil Hitlers' signified or implied mass support. Opposition was penalised by death, torture or imprisonment. To express individuality in word or deed was to run the fatal risk of being accused of treason. In short – self-determination was stifled.

THE GREAT DIVIDE THAT THREATENS WORLD PEACE

In some cultures political and clerical dictatorships have a lot in common; they strive, by years of constant repetition and intimidation, to impose on the minds of vulnerable young people texts and ideologies that are not open to debate, denial, scientific proof or the penetrating light of logic. Such cultures are usually controlled by a media that hides the truth and distorts or misrepresents alternative points of view. The insidious threat being posed under these conditions is not only to the mind but to the emotions as well.

In place of A Rule of Law designed for consistency and transparent justice, there are, in some cultures, laws open to diverse interpretations which facilitate the mental cloning of people who subsequently tend to become convinced that Paradise actually does exist and is worth dying for. This can create a great divide between those who have been conditioned to hold such a belief and an enormous number of people worldwide who regard the notion of Paradise as fiction: nothing more than wishful thinking.

In the Western world a more subtle divide exists between the USA, where Christian Fundamentalism is strongly entrenched, and the more secular countries of Europe. In the USA, political candidates are unlikely to get elected unless they mention God in their speeches. But in secular European countries, including Britain, political candidates are very *unlikely* to get elected if they do.

This intriguing dichotomy illustrates the effect that biased cultures can have on religions and beliefs, and raises a debatable issue: Do we really choose a religion or are so-called beliefs determined largely by geographical factors?

> If you are born or reared in India you are usually Hindu.
> If you are born or reared in a Muslim country you are usually a Moslem.
> If you are born or reared in a Catholic country you are usually a Catholic.
> If you are born or reared in Europe you are likely to be an ex-Catholic or a lapsed Catholic.

Are many religious people really and truly believers, or are they just mentally conditioned followers of various cultures that imbue them with a mindset which discourages independent thought and claims a monopoly of divinely revealed wisdom and truth? Of one thing we can be certain: with so many diverse theological theories and claims to divine revelations of what is true and wise, it is impossible for all of them to be right. One consideration worthy of attention is that a great number of people are hooked into believing things that greatly affect their way of life merely because of where they were born or reared.

Gods and religions of all sorts have come and gone but they have invariably been sustained by fears and superstitions, in contrast to the search for truth about man and the Universe pursued by science.

HANDING OVER YOUR MIND TO BRAINWASHERS

In the final days of WW2 even children of the Hitler Youth organisation were expected to face the terrifying onslaught of Russian armies motivated largely by revenge for atrocities committed against their people.

At a parade, Hitler was photographed as he patted the brainwashed heads of youthful soldiers schooled to kill, as though to praise them for the courage they were expected to show in the dying moments of the Third Reich. The dictator had already robbed these youths of free will, and was about to send many of them to an early death.

Not long after that parade their Fuhrer declared to his dedicated followers:

'If the war is lost, then it is of no concern to me if the people perish in it. I still would not shed a single tear for them, because they did not deserve any better.'

There is a chilling parallel to Hitler's appalling betrayal of his loyal followers. It involved the mass suicide, in 1978, of 914 of the congregation of the so-called People's

Temple Christian Church. Those who were persuaded to take their own lives included nearly 300 children. Jim Jones, their unbalanced leader, had so brainwashed his trusting believers that he was able to talk them into taking a soft drink laced with cyanide and sedatives. They paid a terrible price for allowing someone to take over their lives and deny them the right to do their own thinking.

The awful finale took place at a jungle clearing known as Jonestown in Guyana. Jones, who knew that US lawmen were on their way to arrest him, avoided the agonizing death of loyal followers who had believed him to be honest and sincere. He preferred, like Hitler, to have a bullet in his brain.

Those who escaped (including Deborah Layton, author of an account of life and death in The People's Temple entitled *Seductive Poison*) were belatedly forced to the conclusion that sincerity in a leader is not enough. Many would agree with this; after all, most megalomaniacs are sincere when they deceive others and deceive themselves.

In her riveting book, Deborah Layton cautions all who risk surrendering their minds to an arch deceiver like Jim Jones, or any kind of dictator. She writes:

'Our alarm signals ought to go off as soon as someone tells us their way is the only right way. When our thoughts are forbidden, when our questions are not allowed and doubts are punished. When contacts and friendships outside the organisation are censored, we are being abused for an end that never justifies the means.

***If there is a lesson to be learned it is that an ideal can never be brought about by fear, abuse and the threat of retribution.**[1]*

Abdicating the right of choice

A fundamentalist attitude to politics or religion may suit people who are not able or prepared to think independently, but the example of Jim Jones and his People's Temple Christian Church in the USA serves to prove how dangerous and limiting that can be to mind and spirit, and how important it is to value individuality and freedom of choice.

---

[1] *Seductive Poison* is published in England by Aurum Press Ltd, 25 Bedford Avenue, London. –

SELF-DETERMINATION AND PERSONAL RESPONSIBILITY

Personal responsibility for the murder of an incredible number of people has raised questions in the political case of Stalin. Was he or was he not guilty of causing the deaths of millions of people who opposed his will? He was sane enough to confer rationally with President Roosevelt and Prime Minister Winston Churchill because he 'chose' to act rationally, thereby proving that he could act responsibly when it suited his purpose.

His evil personality may have been due partially to emotional and psychological problems but history is likely to record that he, not his genes, was responsible for the murder of countless valiant and talented Russian people.

The cataclysmic cost of political apathy

After two world wars, costing many millions of lives and causing indescribable bitterness and sorrow, the time has arrived for governments to ensure as far as is possible that political candidates are morally and mentally fit to lead. A democratic system of government does not always provide enough protection against the emergence of a power-mad tyrant; Hitler was democratically elected.

Leaders are not usually chosen because of their moral integrity or emotional maturity. Some acquire power because of a need to compensate for feelings of unworthiness and impotence associated with childhood experiences. As a political opportunist with an aptitude for deception, Hitler found plausible reasons for causing unbelievably horrific deeds by identifying himself with the people he governed. 'I represent the German people and you represent me' was the crux of a repeated statement he made to loyal supporters. This was, in effect, a clue that his personal feelings and delusions were being offloaded on to admirers: who were gradually becoming an extension of himself, warts and all.

When he maintained that Germans were a super race, he was implying that he (an Austrian) was also a super person. His pursuit of power and glory may well have been partially in compensation for the humiliation and shame meted out to him by a bullying, unloving father while his mother looked on, powerless to intervene. But he might also have been genetically predisposed to sadistic behaviour. The world will never know.

Safeguards

Quite clearly, the tactics of people in power, including leaders of great corporations such as owners of influential newspapers and television companies, should be scrutinised by an alert public, backed up by electoral safeguards. Where caution is concerned, the public should not rely too much on media under the financial control of biased capitalists, who should themselves be restrained by safeguards, because the power of their wealth can be a threat to democracy. In

2007 it was disclosed that immediately prior to crucially important political decisions, a British Prime Minister had urgent discussions with a very influential media mogul.

However, full credit should be given to newspaper correspondents and photographers who sometimes risk imprisonment or death in defence of truth and justice abroad; warriors of the word like the journalist Ann Leslie, for example, who campaigns for people everywhere to have political and religious freedom.

GENETIC BARRIERS TO SELF-DETERMINATION

With no immune system, due to a mutated gene, a baby boy could have been killed by the most ordinary infection. But gene therapists at London's Great Ormond Street hospital took bone marrow from him and infused it with a harmless virus that carried the 'correct' gene. To the ecstatic relief of Dr Adrian Thrasher's medical team, the operation was a success. The boy was able to return home with a proper immune system, his capacity for self-determination restored.

Although DNA contains the blueprint that helps to make us what we are, it does not control us completely. We are not, for example, fated to die near the same age as our parents or grandparents; genetic heritage is not an infallible guide to longevity. Medical science and better health care appear to be having a benign influence on the evolutionary blueprint.

Could a mutated gene or brain damage be partially responsible for certain tendencies? C.A.T. scans reveal that the limbic system which controls our emotions is sometimes found to be damaged in paedophiles, causing their emotional system to be wired up wrongly. According to criminologist Colin Wilson, it could cause an inappropriate sexual response: an arousal of sexual interest in children. This may or may not be the case, but it does not rule out the existence of conscience, nor does it rule out the possibility that many people with normal sexual propensities might also have their emotional systems wrongly wired up, but without being similarly affected.

Mozart and Free Will

Was Mozart conditioned by his father to be a genius? Like Beethoven, he was strongly coerced into becoming a superb musician from earliest childhood. But coercion and conditioning could not have produced 50 symphonies, his wonderful Clarinet Concerto, the architectural perfection of Eine Kleine Nachtmusik and his sensational operas.

Like other composers of music, he proved the existence of free will by *choosing* certain keys to suit the mood and style of his compositions. He also set original music to particular rhythms and chose the subjects for his operas. It could be said that he owed a lot to the style of Joseph Haydn, but his unearthly creations are believed by many to be divinely inspired; though he once described himself as '*like a dog with fleas, agitated by creative fits*' that would not allow him to rest.

Whatever the sources of his creativity Mozart was, like everyone, open to influences that affect self-determination: need of money, environment, and social and political situations.

It would be reasonable to assume that, with his remarkable gifts, Mozart had an easy life effortlessly producing the fruits of his genius. But the truth does not bear this out. In his time, composers could not earn money the way pop singers and writers do today because intellectual ownership (copyright) did not exist. Because of this he was often in financial difficulties; forced to travel all over Europe in bumpy, draughty horse-carriages in order to earn commissions for new compositions, and to give piano concerts. This arduous procedure must surely have affected his health and strength considerably. But could he have earned a living in another way? That would have been virtually impossible. Trained and driven by Leopold, his father, Mozart was also impelled by nature and nurture to express his feelings.

In common with all truly original creators of art and music, he proved that free will, within the limitations set by nature and nurture, really does exist.

INFLUENCES THAT CAN AFFECT CAPABILITY

Surrendering your mind to alcohol: the crooked crutch that lets you down

Alcohol continues to stand high on the list of dangerous addictions. Dr Robert Lefever of the Promis Clinic in London estimates that in the UK alone, about 100 people die from the effects of alcohol every day. This statistic is horrifying enough, but records indicate that smoking is even more deadly, causing on average 300 victims every day.

If these figures were to be published often enough, smokers and drinkers of excessive alcohol might begin to take them more seriously, whether in the UK or elsewhere.

The following questions that some addicted people could put to themselves should provide food for thought – thoughts requiring *courage and action:-*

1. Is my habit worth dying for?
2. Do I use alcohol as an escape from something? If so, from what?
3. Why and when did I start to drink excessively?

4. Can I cope in life without smoking, drugs or alcohol? If not, why not?
5. What about those I love and those who depend on me?
6. Should I get psychological help?

Because addicted teenagers appear to figure largely in self-delusion, and because some parents are unwilling or unable to set acceptable standards of behaviour, these situations appear to necessitate preventative education with parent participation on a legally enforced basis.

An American film on alcoholism might have persuaded numerous people to seek psychological help. The film claims that a high percentage of Americans who die under the age of 20 do so because of the effects of alcohol. Relative figures for the U.K. may prove equally alarming. Vulnerable alcohol addicts should perhaps ask themselves some rather obvious questions:

(a) How is my physical, mental and spiritual condition likely to be affected five years from now if I fail to understand and overcome my problems?
(b) How might my social life and career prospects be damaged?
(c) What action is necessary?

Although you may have currently surrendered your mind and body to a crippling addiction, that doesn't mean to say that you can't pick yourself up, brush yourself down and start all over again. Your 'courage' (the first letter in CIA) is not necessarily extinguished: like a smouldering bush fire; it can almost certainly be re-ignited when motivation is found.

The power of words to affect attitudes and moods is common knowledge, and many people have found that the spoken word can affect habits too. Auto-suggestion, like the one on the next page, has enabled some smokers to purge themselves of the habit. Alcoholism can be tackled in the same way; though psychological and social factors should obviously be taken into consideration.

(You need not continue to deplete your life-force)
This method has freed many people from the habit of smoking

Mentally repeat the following auto-suggestion as you envisage going through a typical day as a non-smoker An ideal occasion for doing this is when you are drifting off to sleep.

I have <u>no</u> need and <u>no</u> desire to smoke.

By repeating this auto-suggestion several times daily for a week or more with imagination and determination, you could free yourself from the smoking habit. The suggestion may be equally effective if adapted to alcohol or drugs; provided a person is prepared to avoid the company and influence of addicts.

IN ADDITION TO SMOKING, OTHER WELL-KNOWN DANGERS TO CAPABILITY ARE SOMETIMES IGNORED AT GREAT PERSONAL COST.

DRUG ADDICTION

According to experts who treat drug users regularly, cannabis can impair biological drives and cause mental illness conditions that would certainly affect capability as well. Many users seem to be unaware that cannabis is considered to be much more cancer-causing than tobacco. The London Institute of Drug Dependency has stated that 'Skunk' is just as hallucinogenic as LSD and could, they maintain, lead to a related form of psychosis. These facts have already received publicity but it seems that they cannot be repeated too often.

A United States study claims that female addicts who smoke the drug while pregnant put their children's intellectual development at risk, as well as accelerating their own ageing process.

Some people are more at risk than others to the dangers of cannabis. Users are, in effect, tempting fate: they cannot know how genetically susceptible they may be to moodiness, apathy, paranoia, social incompatibility, memory loss or general incompetence.

As many an addict has discovered, capability can be so impaired by cannabis and other illegal drugs that concentration and motivation may be seriously affected by a laid-back indifference that weakens the desire to succeed and live a full life.

DRUGS IN THE WORKPLACE: THE EFFECTS ON CAPABILITY AND THE VALUE OF SELF-AWARENESS

According to Dr Patrick Dixon, author of *Truth About Drugs*, 80 per cent of big companies in the USA spend more than 200 million pounds (an awful lot of dollars) a year, testing employees for drugs. The reason for this is not hard to find. Drug-takers are, in general:

> 33 % less productive
> three times as likely to be late for work
> four times as likely to hurt themselves or others, and
> ten times more likely to miss work

Random testing in one American company is reported to have brought about a remarkable decrease of 72 % in its accident rate. If this figure is accurate, it implies that an organisation that fails to test employees for drug-taking may be leaving itself open to preventable problems and lower than expected financial returns.

Drug-abusers are not all irresponsible people. They may be very intelligent, with an honest approach to life but harmful self-destructive habits often show that we are not always governed by reason; self-awareness is therefore a priceless asset. This becomes obvious when highly intelligent and capable people behave childishly and irrationally, to the astonishment of friends and neighbours who can sometimes be heard to say: 'I don't know what he/she could have been thinking of; it was completely out of character'.

DRUGS IN THE HOME

The following health education advice has been given to parents:

Talk to children respectfully about their feelings on drugs, making sure your own views and feelings are known. Make them aware that you think they are sensible enough and strong enough not to even experiment with drugs.

*

Set an example. The way you live and behave lets your children know how sincere your attitude toward drugs is. Don't try to pass off cannabis as a harmless recreational substance; let them know how it can have very damaging effects on the chemistry of the brain and can be even more dangerous than tobacco.

*

Make sure you know and meet your children's friends so that you can have some idea of their possible influence.

*

Peer pressure can often be more influential than parental advice. Assess from the conversations and behaviour of your child's friends whether they have knowledge of drug-pushers, but try not to blame or lecture them, difficult though this may be, otherwise you could make them defiant.

*

You may fight shy of getting a drug detector kit, but how can you know if your child is using drugs? An official publication listed the following hints:

> Sudden change of mood, from happy and alert to sullen and moody. .
> Exceptional irritability or aggression
> Loss of appetite
> Loss of interest in hobbies, sport, schoolwork or friends
> Bouts of drowsiness or sleepiness
> Increased evidence of telling lies or furtive behaviour
> Unexplained loss of money or belongings from home
> Unusual smells, stains or marks on the body –or on clothes

*

Children should be made clearly aware that drug-taking is illegal and could lead to trouble with the police.
Some of the above conditions may obviously have nothing to do with drugs, but on the other hand, they might.

Prescribed Drugs: *Can they limit your power to control your life?*

The power or ability to control one's life is under serious threat in the 21st century due to advances in medical manipulation of mind and feeling. Added to this is the widespread use and abuse of so-called recreational drugs that confuse and cloud the mind, causing people to be less capable of establishing a positive mental, physical and spiritual identity, as they lose control of what they think and what they do.

In the opinion of Stephen Rose, author of *The 21st Century Brain,* the more we use drugs such as Ritalin (for attention deficit disorder) and Prozac (for depression) to cure problems rooted in social circumstances, the more likely we shall be to neglect social situations. A highly regarded biologist and writer on genetics, Stephen Rose, is certainly not alone with this opinion.

A Government Health Watchdog warned in 2005 that it isn't just adults who are being prescribed pills as a 'first line' remedy for depression. In 2003 the number of children taking antidepressants was put at 50,000 in the UK alone, but despite a ban on certain antidepressants given to children, there were, according to the British National Institute for Clinical Excellence, 40,000 of them on Prozac in 2005, despite figures indicating that, at best, the drug helps only one in ten depressed youngsters. That organisation has informed doctors that research shows psychological treatments work best and that even children who respond to antidepressants should be offered therapy alongside taking pills.

The argument in favour of psychological treatment in preference to too many pills, put forward by Stephen Rose, is almost certainly pertinent to the unrequited need many young offenders have for mental and emotional contact with their parents– a need that is probably rooted in the financial priority some parents give to home, family and work.

This social and political problem concerning additional help for child or teenage care is surely worthy of more urgent attention in view of the tragic number of teenage suicides in remand homes, and the disproportionate amount of crime committed by young offenders whose positive capabilities in relation to the common good, and to whatever aspirations they might have had, stand very little chance of being developed or realised.

It will never be known how many deaths might have been prevented if only some of the victims' parents had been better able and more prepared to understand, empathise and communicate on an informed level with confused and angry youngsters whose likeability is close to zero – in some cases to a point of no return. But sadly, parenting skills, at a time when they are of vital importance, do not yet have the same priority in schools as history and geography; two subjects that most people can pick up in adult life anyway, through reading, films and many excellent television programmes including superb nature and animal documentaries.

It is not suggested that history and geography should be omitted from the curriculum but that parenting skills could be allocated a portion of the time normally given to these subjects.

SLEEP CAPABILITY AND MEMORY

If you want to confuse and disorientate a political prisoner, deprive that person of sleep and you will almost certainly succeed. It is no surprise that scientists now confirm something the Victorians were well aware of: *sleep can help to make you healthy, wealthy and wise.*

Researchers on the subject published in the journal Neuroscience in 2005 maintain that a good night's sleep improves your memory whereas sleep deprivation can lessen control over emotions, causing stress and anxiety and can act against memory retention, thereby affecting the ability to learn.

Dr Matthew Walker of the Beth Israel Deaconess Medical Centre said:

'When you are asleep it seems as though you are shifting memory to more efficient storing regions within the brain, enabling memory tasks to be carried out more quickly and accurately and with less stress and anxiety'. The American journal Neuroscience also reported that sleeping helps memories to stick in the brain and boosts the ability to learn.

Agoraphobia and capability

Some people are so afraid of open or public spaces that their phobia cuts them off from a world of opportunities on a social and work level. They commit themselves to months or even years of voluntary confinement in their home, rather than trace and face the origin of a fear that renders them incapable of living life to the full. But in some cases CIA and auto-suggestions, such as the one shown overleaf, can help afflicted people back to normality. If, however, their agoraphobia stems from regression to childhood fears, individual psychotherapy may be necessary.

Agoraphobia: an extreme or irrational fear of open or public places

In a casual sort of way

I'll walk further every day

Visualise getting nearer to your destination while you repeat this slogan.
(To be used with or without appropriate therapy)

THE MIND AND THE SOUL

When the famous literary figure Dr Samuel Johnson was insulted in an alehouse because of his small physical stature, he is said to have replied:

> 'Were I so tall to grasp the poles
> and stretch the oceans in my span,
> I must be measured by my soul,
> the mind's the master of the man.'

To Dr Johnson in the eighteenth century, there was no apparent distinction between mind and soul– a view shared by many millions of people in modern times.

Vernon Jordon, a presidential confidant in the Nineties and a very influential American businessman and lawyer, is reported to have said something in 1992 that would probably have delighted Thomas Paine, author of *The Age of Reason*, and also the acerbic Dr Johnson:

> 'I am the custodian of my morality and ethics;
> I am, on that, answerable to myself.'

Like many people, Vernon Jordon identified himself with his own code of ethics in the belief that soul or mind is revealed through a person's behaviour. He was in agreement with Kant, the philosopher who maintained that morality is a product of rational thought; though cannibals could say with equal conviction that standards of morality are sometimes set according to social and geographical circumstances.

The difference between a person who relies on or hopes for help and strength from a god, and a person who depends on himself, is exemplified by the different mental and emotional outlooks of Emily Bronte, author of *Wuthering Heights*, and a relatively obscure poet, W.E.Henley. Although Henley had to spend a long time in hospital while suffering from tuberculosis, he was able to express courage and an 'earthy' spirituality in his inspiring poem 'Invictus', included in one of his books of verse entitled *In Hospital*, which was written in the Edinburgh Royal Infirmary, where he had a leg amputated as a result of the TB. But there was no self-pity or plea for help from a supernatural benefactor.

When Britain stood alone in the Second World War, Winston Churchill quoted Henley's poem during a parliamentary session on September 9, 1941:

Invictus

Out of the night that covers me,
Black as the pit from pole to pole
I thank whatever gods may be
for my unconquerable soul.

In the fell clutch of circumstance
I have not winced nor cried aloud
Under the bludgeonings of chance
My head is bloody but unbowed.

Beyond this place of wrath and tears
Looms but the horror of the shade,
And yet the menace of the years
Finds and shall find me unafraid.

It matters not how strait the gate,
How charged with punishments the scroll,

I am the master of my fate;
I am the captain of my soul.

The very nature of Emily Bronte's religious conditioning caused her to depend on spiritual strength derived from the God depicted in the Bible, in contrast to W.E.Henley and secularists today whose lives centre on self reliance. She and Henley lived in a century dominated by the curse of tuberculosis, but unlike her, he did not believe in the existence of Heaven or Hell and was therefore able to face the inevitability of death in a different way.

Henley's moral courage stemmed from reliance on himself, not on an external power. His never-say-die spirit was admired by Robert Louis Stevenson, author of *Treasure Island,* who based the one-legged pirate Long John Silver on Henley, his courageous one-legged friend.

The Bronte sisters, R. L. Stevenson and countless other victims of the tuberculosis epidemic, so tragically portrayed in the operas of Verdi and Puccini, had to fight with every weapon available to them: a despairing and helpless medical profession; the power within; survival instinct; and belief in an invisible, seemingly indifferent creator.

Emily Bronte's belief in a 'loving and merciful God', did not save the Bronte family from disaster during 1848-9, when Bramwell, her brother, died. Emily and her sister Anne also died of consumption in that period, leaving only Charlotte, stricken by the same illness, to follow them in 1855, to:

> 'Listen to the soft wind
> breathing through the grass
> in that quiet earth.'
> (Lines: by Emily Bronte)

In her poem 'No Coward Soul Is Mine', Emily revealed her attitude to death, implying that her courage to face it stemmed from God's wide, embracing love. Her loyalty to an incomprehensible and remote god might appear these days to have been touchingly naive. But within the god-fearing vicarage where she lived amid windswept Yorkshire Moors, she was probably as out of touch with the influence of humanistic rationality as her stoic and heroic father, a cleric.

DOING IT YOUR WAY

From earliest childhood we are conditioned by the attitudes and the example of our parents. Because of this lots of us could be left wondering whether we recognise and still accept certain characteristics and beliefs as part of our true selves.

The following list may make it easier to trace the origins of certain attitudes and values, and so gain a clearer insight into what is the essential you: which characteristics you are glad you imitated (whether intentionally or not) and which habits, beliefs and values you want to change. (Bear in mind that some characteristics may be genetically endowed)

>Psychological and emotional awareness/lack of awareness
>Harmful addictions
>Good or bad manners
>Love of nature and animals
>Optimism or pessimism
>Determination and persistence
>Kindness and consideration
>Healthy/unhealthy attitude towards sex
>Religious bigotry and political bias

Spiritual or materialistic values
Self-discipline: strong or weak
Confidence or the lack of it
Respect for other people's rights and values
Healthy or unhealthy eating habits

Love and affection or the lack of it
Interest in music, art or sport
Enjoyment of fitness and exercise
Perfectionism/compulsive need for achievement
Respect for law and order
A need to be always right and in control
Humour, fun; a carefree disposition
Hobbies or the lack of them
Patience or impatience
Temper and violence or reasonable control
Unsociable or sociable behaviour
Fear of failure or a bold outlook on life
Lack of imagination
Appreciation of colour and beauty or the lack of it
Generosity or the lack of it
Self-centredness or a concern for and interest in others
Purpose or lack of purpose
Responsible or irresponsible
Carefulness or carelessness with money
Jealousy

Imitation can of course be an effective way of learning, but when imitation is unintended, free will might be restricted insofar as a belief, habit or attitude may not have been considered or analysed. Unintended imitations can stick to us like barnacles below the waterline of ships and the *true* you may remain undetected until brought to light through realisation or circumstance.

One of the main advantages of knowing your true self, as opposed to being the innocent bearer of someone else's habits, beliefs or other characteristics, is that you should be more wary of influencing your children with any undesirable characteristics of your own, such as an unsociable disposition. If, for instance, you are non-tactile and incapable of responding to your child's need for affection, greater self-awareness may prompt you to make up for it by giving your child extra time and attention, and periodic assurances of self-worth.

By attending school parents' evenings you can show that you really care. I have come across a number of people who, when reviewing their childhood, have regretfully remarked on their parents' lack of interest and consideration regarding matters of education and future prospects.

> 'I always hoped they'd turn up for school open day but they seldom did.'

Sometimes, caring, attention and encouragement will be gratefully accepted as a sign of love, even when parents are emotionally unresponsive. More than once I was relieved to hear the remark:

> 'They weren't affectionate but I knew they cared'.

If you discover, from the **true you** list, any attitudes, values, beliefs or habits you wish to lose, CIA, backed up by will power and greater self awareness, should prove very helpful, as may a personal reminder noted on the next page.

Notes

Which, if any, copied attitudes, beliefs or habits am I determined to disown in order to be the real me?

1

2

3

4

5

6

MATERIALISM AND ETHICS

The Indian Ocean seaquake of 2004 snatched something like 300,000 people from their loved ones, including thousands of children. The awesome avalanche of water it caused did not discriminate between believers or non-believers. Even prominent clerics admitted at the time that the catastrophe made them question their faith.

A succession of equally tragic so-called 'acts of God' occur so often as to give the impression that there is no supernatural, all-powerful creator in control, and that if there were, he, she or it could not possibly be loving and caring. With a scenario such as this, where else could anyone look for guidance in a material world?

There really does appear to be a problem for would-be believers in western-type democracies, except in parts of the USA where traditional beliefs appear to be rooted too deep to change in conservative, fundamentalist areas.

In recent times we have been made aware that our DNA bears a fairly close resemblance to the DNA of flies, worms, rats and, of course, our monkey cousins. We are also told that life forms can be duplicated in a laboratory.

This seeming affront to religious theories and dogmas has caused many people to take a more considered, analytical view of the nature and the origin of life forms on planet Earth. Lengthy observations of chimpanzees and other animals have led to the conclusion that some life forms also possess moral attributes.

MORALITY AND CHIMPANZEES

Although chimpanzees are genetically very similar to humans, it is only in recent times that observers have realised just how similar to us they really are, morally and socially, in terms of kindness and consideration.

According to Felix Warneken, research psychologist at the Planck Institute of Evolutionary Anthropology in Leipsig, Germany, chimpanzees sometimes help each other without any thought of personal reward. Altruistic acts appear to be programmed into their genes. In one experiment, a chimpanzee was given the impression that a man, after several attempts, could not stretch far enough to retrieve a stick. The chimpanzee assisted by actually climbing a fence in order to place the stick near to him.

In evolutionary terms, helping a less able member of a species serves to assist in the survival of that species; but altruistic behaviour, unconnected to the survival of genes, has also been observed in dolphins, who have been known to come to the aid of humans in distress at sea; and in wolves, who have brought back meat to members of the pack that did not assist in the kill. It may appear to be stretching a point to suggest that certain species are also capable of empathy! But it does seem that we have underestimated other animals and overestimated our superiority.

In his exciting books, biologist Richard Dawkins has tried to gently distil popular illusions about altruism being a solely human quality. His conclusions on the subject are substantiated by the study of 36 chimpanzees at the Ngamba Island Chimpanzee Sanctuary in Uganda, the results of which were published in June 2007 in The Biology Journal of the Public Library of Science.

Through their unselfish acts of kindness and consideration, verified by various observers and researchers, including Sir David Attenborough, the moral behaviour of some primitive apes indicates that they have genetically conferred on us the rudiments of morality and sociability which we associate with a civil attitude towards our neighbours.

Sigmund Freud might have added that they have also conferred on us the potentialities we try to suppress that lie dormant in the darkest recesses of the mind waiting to be released in times of war. The area he called the Unconscious.

STANDARDS OF ACCEPTABLE CONDUCT

A life with purpose and meaning and a civil attitude towards others in the absence of organised religion is obviously possible: millions of people have proved it. Confucius showed the way 500 years before the arrival of Christianity with a pragmatic, ethical philosophy which included, for example, *'Treat others as you wish to be treated'*, a philosophy that still has influence in China today, where respect for others, a national characteristic, appears to have been imprinted in their DNA.

So how are standards of acceptable conduct satisfactorily maintained without threats of so-called damnation and the restraints of fear? Partly through aspects of civilisation based on each other's rights and needs, and partly through built-in safeguards against anti-social behaviour contained in the Rule of Law.

The legacy of Grecian ethics, which appears to be basic to the western concept of what is right and what is wrong, has been a fundamental influence in establishing standards and boundaries.

So has Christianity, but Christian morality is tied up with belief in the soul and in reward and punishment – a view at variance with many people's sense of reality, especially those who agree with the British biophysicist and Nobel Laureate Francis Crick, who declared:

'Your sense of personal identity and free will are no more than the behaviour of a vast assembly of nerve cells and their associated molecules.'

Many people, including this author, would like to have heard the late Francis Crick's explanation of how the inspired works of Mozart, Beethoven and Shakespeare could have come about within this context.

MATERIALISM

In modern times, the beacon of materialism, within freethinking cultures, twinkles as brightly as the star that guided three wise kings to the city of Bethlehem.

For hundreds of years, while poverty dominated the lives of most people in Europe, giving rise to widespread discontent and disorder, the myths of Heaven, Hell and Paradise provided constant ammunition for clerics who strove to raise standards of behaviour by motivating citizens with reward and punishment incentives. But in time, religion-based fears and superstitions began to lose hold over people in western countries as they became more self sufficient and better informed, thanks largely to the invention of the printing press.

Nowadays, paradise has an alternative meaning. Those who live for the 'here and now' tend to be blissfully materialistic; their paradise consists largely of having a good job, enough money, comfortable accommodation and a good social life.

In opposition to this practical philosophy, there are certain clerical organisations that offer followers heavenly rewards, provided they keep to the stipulated paths of righteousness indicated by their various and sometimes contradictory versions of what is right, what is wrong: what is culturally acceptable and what is not. It must be difficult to specify what those heavenly rewards can possibly be, in view of the fact that no tangible evidence has ever emerged.

WOULD A WORLD WITHOUT RELIGION BE SAFER AND MORE PEACEFUL?

There are good grounds for posing such a question. After all, most wars throughout history have been caused by religious organisations that claim to have exclusive access to some sort of god.

It is no longer acceptable to slaughter human beings on a sacrificial altar as an offering to some supposedly angry god. But in Iraq, opposing theistic zealots have, even in the 21st century, sanctioned the slaughter of thousands of men, women and children of their own sect because of a theological technicality involving the authenticity of various religious practices and beliefs.

The Ancient Greeks had an alternative to this uncivilised behaviour: a moral code based on faith, hope and charity, as well as an appreciation of what is just and good and beautiful. They also valued *humour* and encouraged *tolerance* of other people's views and beliefs. Tolerance and open-mindedness are difficult for fundamentalists because they have closed their minds to alternative opinions, due probably to a fear that they might be proved wrong, in error of judgment or because, in many cases, childhood indoctrination has denied them mental freedom and the right to follow whatever religion or philosophy they might otherwise have chosen.

THE THREE GRACES - FAITH, HOPE AND CHARITY

Although Aristotle did not believe in an afterlife and considered that happiness should be the ultimate goal, he held the view that happiness could not or should not exist without regard to the feelings and rights of others. In his opinion, people marred their chances of happiness by the pursuit of money, power, material possessions and fame.

Could Grecian spiritual values be simply and effectively expressed in sculpture to counter the materialist excesses referred to by Aristotle and Plato? That superb Italian sculptor, Antonio Canova, thought so. He symbolised Grecian spiritual values in his captivating art form The Three Graces, which is commonly presumed these days to portray Faith, Hope and Charity, though the sculpture has in the past also been associated with Youth and Beauty, Mirth and Elegance.

The principles underlying these interpretations can serve as a sturdy bridge across the chasm that might otherwise impair unity between couples who do not share the same religion, and also between those in a situation in which one believes in an afterlife and the other does not.

A mutual standard of values based on an amalgam of Confucian and Grecian ethics, from which Christian teachings were partially derived, is the bedrock upon which Western civilisation precariously rests.

Some people might say that Canova's sculpture The Three Graces is more admired and valued than the virtues it represents. Yet when we bring those virtues to life they can make us more likeable, more lovable and, indirectly, more capable. Many of us are not noticeably virtuous, but we are inclined to like and respect those who are, because:

Faith in oneself can combat various fears, apathy, arrogance, ignorance, emotional insecurity and lack of courage.
Hope can lessen envy, indifference, despair, ignorance, pessimism, procrastination and self-imposed limitations.
Charity, an aspect of **Love**, can discourage hate, cruelty, intolerance, selfishness, vengeance, meanness and greed - while encouraging their opposites.

A big advantage of aspiring to Faith, Hope and Charity is that these universal values are not linked with reward, punishment, ritual or dogma, but to peace of mind, kindness and a life that is harmonious and balanced.

Harmonious and balanced materialists

It is of course possible to live a life that is harmonious and balanced whether one is motivated religiously or by atheistic principles. Some people may think that a happy medium is a clairvoyant who has won a jackpot; but happy mediums are to be found everywhere. They are people who achieve materialistic moderation and are able to express themselves in the humane way that Mr and Mrs C did while on holiday in the Azores.

The following is an account of an article in a London newspaper. An emaciated stray puppy followed Mr and Mrs C on an eight-hour journey across a volcanic lake and up a steep mountainside, falling behind every now and then through sheer exhaustion. The Portuguese Point pup, with protruding ribs, was in a deplorable condition; but not any more. Mr and Mrs C got the poor creature medical attention and brought it back with them to England, at a personal cost of £4000.

Their earthy spirituality goes back a long way in human history, perhaps to the first time a savage caveman or woman handed a weaker non-hunter member of the tribe a portion of his or her meal. Civilisation is associated with many things, including politeness and good manners; and it certainly owes a lot to kindness and generosity.

Moral Guidance: The Humanist View

Collins Concise Dictionary describes humanists as people who believe they can lead a good life without religious or superstitious beliefs.

Humanists hold the view that this is the only life we have; that it is not a preparation for another life after death, and that it is up to those who believe in life after death and the existence of Paradise to prove it.

Humanists tend to share many values with religious people but prefer to be guided in the quest for social harmony and general happiness by reason and compassion rather than look for so-called divine guidance.

The Three Graces

The splendid life size group sculpture of the Three Graces was installed under Canova's supervision at Woburn Abbey in 1819. It was later purchased for the nation and can now be seen, periodically, at the Victoria and Albert museum in Kensington, London.

An earlier marble carving intended for Empress Josephine the estranged wife of Napoleon Bonaparte is in the Hermitage, St Petersburg.

DOES LIFE HAVE A PURPOSE?

E.O.Wilson, an internationally respected expert in biological science, has forecast that:

'a new morality will emerge from insights of evolutionary biology and genetics and that ultimately, science will replace religion'.

This may seem highly improbable to many people but already in the western world, biological science and evolutionary theory offer the possibility of a complete account of human life - without reference to any sort of extraterrestrial entity.

Yet despite this, millions of people still retain a measure of hope and feel a need to believe that in some way they will continue to exist after death. Nonetheless, blind faith alone cannot forever silence such questions as:

Q. Why am I here on Earth?
A. Because (a biologist might answer) the human species is a link in an evolutionary chain stretching back many millions of years during which

innumerable species have come and gone.

Q. Has life no purpose except survival?
A. To quote the brilliant columnist Val Hennessy of London's Daily Mail newspaper:

'Most of us want to believe we are more than temporary arrangements of nerve cells and molecules, that our personality persists after closing time.'

And, true to say, most of us cherish the thought that we are in some way rather special, but an answer to the question: 'Has life no purpose'? is, of course, one that each of us has to decide for ourselves.

Forms of life evolve and mutate in response to various circumstances and conditions: conditions such as the distance of the Earth from the sun - which determines where and whether life forms can exist.

William Shakespeare seemed to think that we take life too seriously, judging by his remark that *'Life is a tale told by an idiot, signifying nothing'*.

Q. If life has no meaning, why should we bother to have moral standards?
A. Consider the alternatives. People who lie, kill, cheat and steal, with no consideration for others, are liable to finish up behind bars, or lead a friendless, unhappy existence. A moral life, on the other hand, tends to make a person more likeable or lovable because it implies a degree of selflessness and concern for the needs and rights of others.

Where does this leave anyone who needs the framework of a moral discipline yet does not believe in an all powerful creator? Peter Conradi thinks that Buddhism may be the answer. In his book *Going Buddhist*, he implies that Buddhism is tailor-made for those in need of a system of godless belief because it proposes a way of not eradicating ego, but of ceasing to live *exclusively* from within the narrow perspective that ego offers.

Meditation, he believes, can give you a still and accepting mind, which cultivates patience and reveals a person's concealed business, promoting wellbeing and compassion for others.

Is death the end of us?

A definitive answer appears to lie beyond the limits of human understanding, but whatever the truth of the matter, it may be that after death we shall continue to exist in the memories and feelings of those we have loved and befriended. We shall survive, in a sense, through the genes we pass on and through selfless acts and deeds of courage that have helped to enrich and preserve the best that civilisation has to offer.

Ethical materialists

Capitalists, whether religious or not, do apparently need a *purpose* that transcends materialism and the profit motive. At the time of writing, a pro-capitalist newspaper in England, The Sunday Times, has focused attention on blindness. The paper initiated a campaign in 2006 in aid of millions of sightless people in the developing world, stressing that much of this affliction which devastates so many lives is preventable or reversible, and invited readers to make contributions to ease the pitiable condition of people who cannot help themselves. Another capitalist organisation, the Standard Chartered Bank, contributed over a million pounds to help the sightless, but also, presumably, to show that they are a caring bank.

Whatever the motive for giving, the main criterion should be that someone in need should benefit. Formerly, this sort of action to ameliorate the plight of suffering and disadvantaged people would have been shouldered largely by religious organisations but the acceptable face of secularism now frequently rises above material priorities as many affluent people look further than themselves.

Robert Byrne, a Scottish poet, was apparently of the opinion that through active involvement in the course of a lifetime, we can and should find our own reason for living. He wrote:

> *'The purpose of life – is a life of purpose.'*

Ask any proud mother whether she has a purpose in life, as she bills and coos to her baby, and she may give you a questioning, bemused look: as though to say: 'Isn't it obvious?'

Untold millions of women have found life worth living through the joys and responsibilities of motherhood - so much so that a high percentage of them have chosen not to return to well paid, prestigious jobs.

People who lack purpose may have only themselves to

blame if they have been too timid to risk the responsibility of having a family or of accepting the sorts of responsibilities that can give spice and purpose to life.

A job with a purpose does not necessarily involve a lofty ideal. A well-known football manager once implied that a job is as important or as meaningful as you care to make it. His much quoted saying was:

> 'Football is not just a matter of life or death; it's more important than that.'

A purpose in life can relate to anything that is interesting and worthwhile. A prominent industrialist enquired on his deathbed whether his firm's shares were up or down. He was assured, truthfully or untruthfully, that his shares had risen in value. The contented materialist then died, it was said, with a smile on his face. Like millions of others, he had found a purpose in living by expressing his talents and satisfying his needs.

It is worth recalling that when bombs were raining down on London during the Second World War and values were brought into question because life was under constant threat, Ivor Novello wrote a smash hit song entitled

'Love is My Reason for Living'.

Finding meaning and a purpose through experiences

Circumstances such as denial of freedom or a threat to physical survival tend to widen a person's perspective on what life has to offer and what it means. In 1914 the future for millions of the unemployed looked bleak, and lamentably predictable. This caused men to flock to army recruitment centres, not only to show their patriotism in time of war, but to take advantage of an opportunity to discover their true worth. After horrendous experiences, and the daily endurance of mud and blood in the trenches, peace in 1918 brought them face-to-face with the same unpromising existence they had once known.

The status quo was still loaded against so-called working-class people in terms of opportunities and rewards, but the time had arrived when they were no longer prepared to tolerate social injustices that restricted many of them to menial, purposeless tasks. This applied particularly to women who had toiled in war factories and participated in every area of combat. Through the Suffragettes' organised protests, they irresistibly asserted their right to vote.

Fulfilment through work

Not everyone feels a need for a spiritual purpose in life, especially if they are emotionally fulfilled. The renowned physicist Richard Feynman found sufficient motivation in his work. He said:

'I don't feel frightened by not knowing things, by being lost in a mysterious universe without having any purpose, which is the way it really is so far as I can tell. It doesn't frighten me.'

Is it possible, during the course of work, for a naturalist to change the way people think, and even affect their beliefs? Prior to the publication of Charles Darwin's sensational book *On the Origin of the Species*, the answer would most likely have been a resounding 'no'. However, filled with purpose but also seeking meaning and truth through the work he was doing, Darwin did indeed change the way many people think and believe through his theory on Natural Selection, which implied that it was the survival of the aptest (smartest and most able) over *millions* of years (rather than the 6000 years implied in the Christian Bible) that gave rise to the phenomenon of the human race.

Although a practising Christian, Darwin had to come to the reluctant conclusion that mankind was not created by an all-powerful god for a special purpose, but is one of innumerable species in the evolutionary chain. It is claimed and believed by a great number of people that his theory is corroborated by the record of evolutionary history contained in DNA, which we genetically share with other animals – the DNA link being deoxyribonucleic acid, a substance present in nearly all living organisms.

Individuality and environment

When certain people inherit a hand-me-down faith, they may be disinclined to question it as long as they feel mentally and emotionally secure within its structure and as long as it provides a semblance of meaning and purpose. This attitude is sometimes adopted by those who wish to identify with their parent's wishes and customs, like the Christian group in North America known as The Old Order Amish Mennonite Church, which settled in Pennsylvania in the 18th century. They shun modern forms of communication and wear unfashionable clothing reminiscent of bygone years. Their children may or may not be happy to continue traditional customs of an extreme nature but to all appearances, free will appears to have been side-tracked because of the environment in which they were raised.

The same could be said of children reared in other fundamentalist communities; or, indeed, children from very conservative families who are discouraged from expressing initiative, choice or individuality because of obdurate parental attitudes. But it is important for parents to note that DNA proves how different we all are and that obligatory conformity to tradition and customs can be a restriction on free will, self-determination, the expression of talents, and the development of an individual personality.

Notes

My Main Purpose in Life

Attained	To be attained

CHOOSING A SUITABLE PARTNER

Some Japanese dating agencies have a very down-to-earth attitude when it comes to matching up their clients. They compare blood groups in order to check biological compatibility, the assumption being that there is a connection between cells and personality. This may seem to be an unromantic approach to a romantic situation, but it is widely accepted that genes can and do influence behaviour to a certain extent.

In support of this theory, some recipients of donated human organs have reported changes in their choice of foods and in their behaviour, the implication being that they have become influenced by their donor's cell memories. We can either believe or disbelieve them, the evidence being of a personal nature.

In Europe and the USA precautions against marital mismatches do not seem to go much further than the detection or prevention of hereditary or transmitted diseases, but in this DNA era genetic features are likely to receive more attention if the matching of blood groups leads to a sophisticated medical analysis of characteristics contained or assumed to be contained in people's blood cells. Such steps would presumably make very little difference to those who are determined to commit to a partnership. But gene scrutiny might help to cut down the number of one-parent families if inadvisable liaisons could be fairly accurately predicted.

Blood groups, according to the Japanese theory, indicate the following characteristics:

Blood types:

- O Strong survival instinct, drive, leadership qualities, decisiveness, optimistic but selfish and arrogant.
- A Adaptable and considerate, bottles up stress and is oversensitive to criticism.
- B Balanced personality; harmony in relationships.
- AB Unsettled individuals: prone to conflict.

Dr Peter D'Adams, author of *Eat Right Diet*, appears to give support to the Japanese theory; he is of the opinion that we have different emotional, nutritional and health needs according to blood groups. But despite that, anyone involved in matching up couples according to their blood group would need to be able to differentiate between the 'blood group' effect and the 'nurture' effect because even though there may be a perfect blood match, one proposed partner might be an emotionally insecure individual from a dysfunctional family environment, dominated by an unquenchable need to be loved and cared for. So what can be done about the risk of making an unwise choice?

I offer the following tentative suggestion to anyone looking for a mate:

Try to be lucky enough to partner someone who has been loved in childhood, especially by the parent of the opposite sex, otherwise you may find that your partner unconsciously transfers negative reactions on to you. For example, some people whose parents could not or would not show affection are themselves very wary of giving affection or of trusting anyone.

It could be argued that if you genuinely love someone, you should love them for their imperfections as well as their virtues; that marriages or partnerships often flourish on differences and problems. But on the other hand, one cannot ignore the number of separations arising from differences and problems that might have been avoided if only counselling or psychotherapy had been utilized beforehand or as soon as problems started. A pre-marital counsellor might emphasise, for example, the importance of thinking carefully before committing to a prospective partner who is irresponsible with money, in view of the fact that a worrying percentage of marriages do break up because of money problems. The trouble is that most people do not consult anyone about incompatibilities of such seeming insignificance prior to legalising a partnership.

Preventative measures

It might be a good idea to make a note of pitfalls that have occurred in the relationships of your parents or married friends and colleagues. A difficulty you may particularly wish to avoid (but which is frequently encountered by marriage counsellors) is choosing a partner who is not emotionally prepared for the responsibilities of family life.

Another obstacle to happiness and harmony can be what is commonly known as 'a clash of personalities', where one partner, for example, cannot or will not acknowledge the other's individuality and is bent on taking control, or when one partner likes travelling and the other prefers to stay where they are, or where one is sociable and the other is not, etc.

The Jewel in the Crown

If you don't know whether you are in love or whether you want to risk a long-term partnership, 'empathy' might provide the answer, because without it, your relationship would be unlikely to last.

Empathy is a capacity and willingness to imagine oneself in another's place and understand the other's feelings, ideas and actions. If this desirable quality is absent in either party it may be due to a lack of sincerity, an unwillingness to commit on a serious level: unworthy intentions based on money or status – or even because either part may be insufficiently mature for the responsibilities that a profound relationship entails.

Such a situation could invalidate any prior conclusions reached regarding genetic compatibility or blood groups.

OBSTACLES TO BEAR IN MIND

1.

2

3

4

5

6

PART FIVE

THE BEST WAY TO LIVE

In his book *The Best Way to Live*, A. C. Grayling speculates on the ideal way of living a good life. In his view, a good life is a considered life, free, creative, informed and chosen, a life of achievement and fulfilment, of pleasure and understanding, of love and friendship: in short, the best life in a human world lived humanely.

(A case history)

Mr D, undergoing psychotherapy, would probably have regarded this hypothesis as unrealistic because it appears to suppose that a person is free in mind, body and spirit. But he was certainly not free of dependence on his mother or of her dependence on him. He was, therefore, unable to live according to A.C.Grayling's optimistic and hopeful formula.

'I seem to be powerless to do anything about my position,' he said, seething with frustration. Mr D was told the tale of an elephant that assumed it was incapable of breaking free from a chain fixed to a stake in the ground, until one day the giant creature, *imagining* itself breaking away from captivity, gave the chain a sharp tug, and was immediately free.

The shackle that tethered Mr D to his mother was composed largely of fears: fear that his mother would disapprove of him leaving her for another woman, and fear that she would not be able to cope now that her husband was dead. Therapy helped him to summon the strength to break free of dependence on his mother.

'You're not doing your mother any favours by continuing to live with her,' he was told. 'In fact she's likely to become more self-sufficient and sociable when she's not relying on your company.'

Mr D was advised to visualise enquiring at estate agents and to visit locations where he'd like to live. He was reminded, too, of the importance of setting a time limit in case his resolve weakened. Another part of a 'self-assertion programme' was to look for and accept further opportunities to express his independence so that he was no longer passed over when occasions for promotion arrived. Accepting reasonable and worthwhile risks, he was told, can be a sign of maturity of mind and spirit; by acting like an independent person, he would be establishing his adult status and gain enough confidence to tell his mother 'I've found my own place and I'm leaving'. He was introduced to self-hypnosis as a means of reinforcing a determination to be free, and was reminded of the power of visualisation: how it can add another dimension to hypnotic suggestions such as 'I can and I will get a home of my own'. He was given the following hints about self-conditioning:

A semi-hypnotic state can be brought about by being quietly relaxed as, with eyes closed, you think:
1. My feet are feeling as heavy as a block of wood.
2. This heaviness is going up my legs and up my body to my neck.

3. All the nerves and muscles of my neck and my head are becoming more relaxed.
4. My breathing is getting slower and deeper – as in normal sleep.
5. Think: On the count of five, I will be completely relaxed, concentrating entirely on auto-suggestions that are short, positive and reasonable.

To exit the altered state of consciousness, think: On the count of six, I will open my eyes and be fully alert.

Suggestions should ideally be positive, beginning with something like:

I will, I shall, I can, or I am...

Two or three minutes of repetition for several days can prove very effective when the aim is reasonable and feasible. Visualisation, as previously emphasised, gives suggestions a stronger imprint.

A PORTRAIT OF A POPULAR AND POSITIVE PERSON

In sharp contrast to Mr D is the following portrait of a more fortunate person who was lucky enough to have parents who encouraged his natural endeavours, regardless of whether they approved of them.

Although frustrated by dyslexia, a condition that barred him from academic achievement at school, he was intuitively able to compensate for an inability to write or read words and sentences as easily as others do, by utilising the power of life's driving forces and by positively maximising innate qualities, such as leadership and initiative.

So well did the young Mr P respond to life's challenges that he has become an icon in the world of business. It is as though he is driven by gene power to be a super 'doer'. On the surface, he appears to be a dedicated materialist yet to him, money is apparently incidental to the expression of a constant need for risk and achievement.

He appears to epitomise most of what A. C. Grayling outlines in his version of 'the best way to live'.

Whether or not material success brings contentment

depends, of course, on expectations and values, and the extent to which life is enriched by friendships and love. But Mr P seems to regard contentment as a state of mind more suited to cows; he is, seemingly, motivated by excitement and change.

From his parents he apparently learnt the value of self-discipline, responsibility and self-belief; qualities that have helped him to align instinctive and genetic potentialities with his chosen way of life. Mr P does appear to have found *his* best way to live, through striving courageously with bulldog tenacity to reach chosen objectives, though the majority of adults could also claim to have shared what was presumably his most meaningful experience: rearing a family.

To be rich and powerful yet popular at the same time is quite an achievement, but Mr P manages it with a smile while fighting tooth and nail in the business jungle. So how does he cope with an enormous workload without being exhausted and grim? Whether consciously or not, he utilises innate resources very positively. Instincts, for instance, are like units of power and direction that may be used wisely or unwisely, consciously or unconsciously, as details of the following natural drives indicate:

Sex and tenderness: Mr P appears to have been emotionally sustained and balanced by loving, supportive parents as well as by his own family.

Acquisitiveness: Squirrels secrete nuts to safeguard against leaner times. Maybe Mr P collects businesses for the same reason; though of course, other motives and aims are obviously involved.

The social or herd instinct: which inclines hyenas, lions, wolves and other animals to hunt in packs has evolved into such a state of sophistication in human affairs that if you are not socially cooperative you may be regarded as a loner or stand-offish. Even if you are positive in other ways, you are unlikely to be popular with colleagues if you are not reasonably affable in human company, for whatever reason.

Mr P expresses the social instinct to very good effect, which is just as well because nearly all his businesses depend on good public relationships. If he had been morose and remote, not complying with his social instinct, there would have been a different story to tell.

Aggression or Self-assertion: Unpretentious and virtually classless, Mr P has a casual and friendly approach; but of necessity in the business world he is not without guile. A steely resolve, combined with these characteristics, helps to make him a persuasive, influential pack leader, able to use people as other employers do, but in the nicest possible way. However, realising as he apparently does, that being brainy and acceptable is largely genetic, he is accordingly modest about achievements and successes: elite but not elitist.

POPULARITY AND CHARACTER

The following list of desirable characteristics was contributed by readers of a woman's magazine in answer to the question 'What would you ideally wish for in a partner?' The list is in random order:

1. Relaxed and friendly - not a show-off
2. Broad minded; not dogmatic about beliefs
3. Interesting to talk to: a good listener
4. Reasonably generous - not selfish
5. Truthful and reliable
6. Kind, understanding and respectful
7. Affectionate, thoughtful and loyal
8. Someone close to nature: not too materialistic
9. A sense of humour
10. Good with children and animals
11. Ethical values
12. A person with grown-up feelings
13. Not envious, jealous or devious
14. Someone who values me, regardless of my looks
15. Someone who is mentally strong
16. A person who is not a miser or a spendthrift
17. Respects my individuality and my opinions
18. Has interests and hobbies

It was mendacity that toppled one particular U.S. President. He was knowledgeable, intelligent, experienced, dedicated to duty, and had been voted into office with an overwhelming majority, but because he proved to be untruthful he was dismissed from the highest office in the land.

Readers of the woman's magazine who supplied the list of desirable characteristics were apparently in agreement with Greek philosophers that 'truth' really is a primary virtue. Women may not claim to be always truthful themselves, but it is a virtue they would presumably look for in the father of their children.

Noticeably, sexual attraction and good looks did not receive a mention. Perhaps suitors try to go deeper than first impressions now that so many partnerships fail to last the course.

As well as using the above list - evaluating desirable characteristics in other people, it might be revealing and useful to ask yourself how many of them you can claim to possess and whether there is anything in the list that might enhance your L and Lo.

Notes

Characteristics I possess   Characteristics I desire to acquire

HUMOUR AND POPULARITY

If you are blessed with a sense of humour, don't waste it, spread it around. It may brighten the lives of others - and they will like you for it. Of all the things that endear and bind people together, humour, as the Ancient Greeks realised, has a special place. It can take the sting out of an argument, ease pain and, according to Dr Peter Hanson's book *Joy of Stress*, it can even improve resistance to disease, help you to forget your woes and defend you against stresses.

Jewish people have faced more than their fair share of jokes and abuse but they have stoically directed their own special brand of humour against themselves. A typical example of Jewish humour goes as follows:

> Q. What's the difference between a Rottweiler and a Jewish mother?
> A. A Rottweiler eventually lets go.

Even when jokes rise up from the pit of despair, as happened during WW2, and from hospital patients, they seem to have an alleviating effect.

When the greatly loved actor comedian Snozzle Durante

was mugged, one of his assailants suddenly recognised the man who had made him laugh. The villain apologised profusely and returned all he had taken. Mr Durante's response is not recorded, which is a pity because he was such a humorous character. But with his husky voice and wall-to-wall smile he might have said something like: 'Gee! Tanks a millyun; sure you wouldn't like sumut fer ye favourite charity?' Snozzle, like numerous other comedians, proved that humour, like music and sport, has no boundaries and costs nothing, yet it lightens the human lot.

British audiences were hugely relaxed and entertained by the face and farce of comedian Tommy Cooper who liked to make fun of himself as a magician. His most sensational show was when he died during a performance. Everyone thought he was kidding. But long after he left us, his jokes still bring laughter and smiles. A typical corny gag of his was:

'I got home I could hear the phone ringing so I raced upstairs, I picked it up and said: "Hello, who's speaking?" a voice answered: "You are."'

Diarist Samuel Pepys said: 'Singing doth fill the lungs and make the heart feel good.' The same can surely be said of humour and laughter.

Obituary columns of national newspapers inform us of the passing of many famous people; but how many are sorely missed, compared with comedians who have brought us joy and laughter?

A sense of humour may be genetically bestowed or encouraged by one's upbringing, but anyone who cannot express humour need not despair; our four-legged friends prove how other attributes can bring fun and popularity. If we could be even half as friendly and cheerful as man's age-long companion the dog, we'd have all the friends we could cope with. They know when we are sad or unwell and they want us to be as carefree and as glad as they are. They are loyal, openly affectionate, –uncomplaining (when treated with kindness), fun loving, not usually malicious: and they offer lifelong trust and companionship. No wonder they are popular.

Whether or not they have a sense of humour is open to debate. But cats, known for being independent and selfish, as well as charming and beautiful, are not, in my experience, without a sense of humour.

A couple of Burmese cats used to boss our neighbourhood, entering cat flaps at will. One night, while half asleep, I felt a sharp nip on my big toe, which apparently protruded above the blanket. As the cat flap closed with a clatter, I saw the intruders swaggering up the garden path, probably with a satisfied grin.

ENCOURAGING WORDS

Encouragement costs nothing but it can have magical effects that may last a lifetime. The Wizard of Oz knew that a few encouraging words can inspire, stimulate, revitalize, create hope and increase self-belief. He appears to have relied on them quite a lot in order to maintain his reputation as a wise and powerful wizard.

Lack of comforting support in needful times might have motivated the lyricist of one of the most popular songs of all time:-

Home on the Range
(First verse)
Oh give me a home where the buffalo roam,
Where the deer and the antelope play,
Where seldom is heard a discouraging word
And the sky is not clouded all day.
(Words by Brewster Higley, music by Dan Kelly)

The legendary Wicked Witch of the West would presumably have got great pleasure from the use of ***dis***couraging words, being well aware how seriously they can affect a person's courage and confidence.

ADVICE FROM ROBERT LOUIS STEVENSON

Robert Louis Stevenson, author of *Treasure Island*, *Kidnapped*, and *Dr Jekyll and Mr Hyde* outlined a personal view on the best way to live:

1. Make up your mind to be happy: learn to find pleasure in simple things.
2. Make the best of your circumstances. No one has everything, and everyone has something of sorrow intermingled with the gladness of life. The trick: make laughter outweigh the tears.
3. Don't take yourself too seriously. Don't think that somehow you should be protected from misfortunes that befall others.
4. You can't please everybody: don't let criticism hurt you.
5. Don't let your neighbours set your standards; be yourself.
6. Do the things you enjoy doing, but always stay out of debt.
7. Don't borrow trouble: 'imaginary' things are harder to bear than the actual ones.
8. Since hate poisons the soul, don't cherish

enmities or grudges: avoid people who make you unhappy.
9. Have many interests: if you can't travel, read about new places.
10. Don't hold post-mortems. Don't spend your life brooding over sorrows or mistakes. Don't be the one who never gets over things.
11. Do what you can for those less fortunate than yourself.
12. Keep busy at something: a busy person never has time to be unhappy.

Some people might think that R. L. Stevenson probably found it easy to be so magnanimous, kind of heart and forgiving; that he probably didn't have too much to trouble him. But like so many people of his time he was a victim of tuberculosis. That worthy man died of the disease in Samoa, where he had gone in the hope of attaining better health.

**Many people equate success
with wealth and achievement
however, you may be successful —
or may be not; but the final test
is whether you have loved
and whether you have
done your best.**

(Anthony Jones)

BIBLIOGRAPHY

Appleyard, B. (2000). Brave New Worlds. Harper Collins.

Benson, N.C. & Bonn Van Loon. (2003). Introducing Psychotherapy. Icon Books.

Conrad, P. (2004). Going Buddhist. Short.

Darwin, C. (1982). On the Origin of Species. Penguin.

Darwin, C. (1999). The Expression of the Emotions in Man and Animals. Harper Collins.

Dawkins, R. (1976). The Selfish Gene. Oxford University Press.

Dawkins, R. (1986). The Blind Watchmaker. Harlow: Longman.

D'Adams, P. (1998). Eat Right Diet. Century.

Farquharson, M. (2001). Complementary Therapies. Harper & Collins.

Frankl, V. (1985). Man's Search for Meaning. Washington Square Press.

Grayling, A.C. (2004). The Best Way to Live. Orion.

Greenfield, S. (1994). The Human Brain. Weidenfeld & Nicolson.

Harrison, T. (1994). Stigmata. Fount.

Harris, J. (1998). The Nurture Assumption. Bloomsbury.

Hanson, P. (1988). The Joy of Stress. Pan McMillan.

Harrold, F. (2005). Indestructible Self Belief. Piatkins.

Layton, D. (1999). Seductive Poison. Aurum Press.

Morgan, P. (2000). Marriage Lite: The Rise of Cohabitation. Civitas.

Rowan, J. (1998). The Reality Game. Routledge.

Russell, B. (1989). The Conquest of Happiness. Allen & Unwin.

Wilson, E.O. (2002). On Human Nature. Harvard University Press.

Winston, R. (2002). Human Instinct. Bantam Books.